Organization Development: Change Stratgies

James Hammons, Editor

NEW DIRECTIONS FOR COMMUNITY COLLEGES

Sponsored by the ERIC Clearinghouse for Junior Colleges

ARTHUR M. COHEN, *Editor-in-Chief*
FLORENCE B. BRAWER, *Associate Editor*

Number 37, March 1982

Paperback sourcebooks in
The Jossey-Bass Higher Education Series

Jossey-Bass Inc., Publishers
San Francisco • Washington • London

Organization Development: Change Strategies
Volume X, Number 1, March 1982
James Hammons, *Editor*

New Directions for Community Colleges Series
Arthur M. Cohen, *Editor-in-Chief*; Florence B. Brawer, *Associate Editor*

New Directions for Community Colleges (publication number USPS 121-710)
is published quarterly by Jossey-Bass Inc., Publishers, in association with
the ERIC Clearinghouse for Junior Colleges. *New Directions* is numbered
sequentially — please order extra copies by sequential number. The volume
and issue numbers above are included for the convenience of libraries.
Second-class postage rates paid at San Francisco, California, and at additional
mailing offices.

The material in this publication was prepared pursuant to a contract with
the National Institute of Education, U.S. Department of Health, Education,
and Welfare. Contractors undertaking such projects under government
sponsorship are encouraged to express freely their judgment in professional
and technical matters. Prior to publication, the manuscript was submitted
to the Center for the Study of Community Colleges for critical review and
determination of professional competence. This publication has met such
standards. Points of view or opinions, however, do not necessarily represent
the official view or opinions of the Center for the Study of Community
Colleges or the National Institute of Education.

Correspondence:
Subscriptions, single-issue orders, change of address notices, undelivered
copies, and other correspondence should be sent to *New Directions*
Subscriptions, Jossey-Bass Inc., Publishers, 433 California Street,
San Francisco, California 94104.

Editorial correspondence should be sent to the Editor-in-Chief,
Arthur M. Cohen, at the ERIC Clearinghouse for Junior Colleges,
University of California, Los Angeles, California 90024.

Library of Congress Catalogue Card Number LC 81-48473

International Standard Serial Number ISSN 0194-3081

International Standard Book Number ISBN 87589-883-1

Cover art by Willi Baum
Manufactured in the United States of America

This publication was prepared with funding from the National Institute of
Education, U.S. Department of Health, Education, and Welfare under
contract no. 400-78-0038. The opinions expressed in the report do not
necessarily reflect the positions or policies of NIE or HEW.

Ordering Information

The paperback sourcebooks listed below are published quarterly and can be ordered either by subscription or as single copies.

Subscriptions cost $35.00 per year for institutions, agencies, and libraries. Individuals can subscribe at the special rate of $21.00 per year *if payment is by personal check.* (Note that the full rate of $35.00 applies if payment is by institutional check, even if the subscription is designated for an individual.) Standing orders are accepted.

Single copies are available at $7.95 when payment accompanies order, and *all single-copy orders under $25.00 must include payment.* (California, Washington, D.C., New Jersey, and New York residents please include appropriate sales tax.) For billed orders, cost per copy is $7.95 plus postage and handling. (Prices subject to change without notice.)

To ensure correct and prompt delivery, all orders must give either the *name of an individual* or an *official purchase order number.* Please submit your order as follows:

Subscriptions: specify series and subscription year.
Single Copies: specify sourcebook code and issue number (such as, CC8).

Mail orders for United States and Possessions, Latin America, Canada, Japan, Australia, and New Zealand to:

Jossey-Bass Inc., Publishers
433 California Street
San Francisco, California 94104

Mail orders for all other parts of the world to:

Jossey-Bass Limited
28 Banner Street
London EC1Y 8QE

New Directions for Community Colleges Series
Arthur M. Cohen, *Editor-in-Chief*
Florence B. Brawer, *Associate Editor*

CC1 *Toward a Professional Faculty,* Arthur M. Cohen
CC2 *Meeting the Financial Crisis,* John Lombardi
CC3 *Understanding Diverse Students,* Dorothy M. Knoell
CC4 *Updating Occupational Education,* Norman C. Harris
CC5 *Implementing Innovative Instruction,* Roger H. Garrison
CC6 *Coordinating State Systems,* Edmund J. Gleazer, Jr., Roger Yarrington
CC7 *From Class to Mass Learning,* William M. Birenbaum
CC8 *Humanizing Student Services,* Clyde E. Blocker
CC9 *Using Instructional Technology,* George H. Voegel
CC10 *Reforming College Governance,* Richard C. Richardson, Jr.
CC11 *Adjusting to Collective Bargaining,* Richard J. Ernst
CC12 *Merging the Humanities,* Leslie Koltai

CC13 *Changing Managerial Perspectives,* Barry Heermann
CC14 *Reaching Out Through Community Service,* Hope M. Holcomb
CC15 *Enhancing Trustee Effectiveness,* Victoria Dzuiba, William Meardy
CC16 *Easing the Transition from Schooling to Work,* Harry F. Silberman, Mark B. Ginsburg
CC17 *Changing Instructional Strategies,* James O. Hammons
CC18 *Assessing Student Academic and Social Progress,* Leonard L. Baird
CC19 *Developing Staff Potential,* Terry O'Banion
CC20 *Improving Relations with the Public,* Louis W. Bender, Benjamin R. Wygal
CC21 *Implementing Community-Based Education,* Ervin L. Harlacher, James F. Gollattscheck
CC22 *Coping with Reduced Resources,* Richard L. Alfred
CC23 *Balancing State and Local Control,* Searle F. Charles
CC24 *Responding to New Missions,* Myron A. Marty
CC25 *Shaping the Curriculum,* Arthur M. Cohen
CC26 *Advancing International Education,* Maxwell C. King, Robert L. Breuder
CC27 *Serving New Populations,* Patricia Ann Walsh
CC28 *Managing in a New Era,* Robert E. Lahti
CC29 *Serving Lifelong Learners,* Barry Heermann, Cheryl Coppeck Enders, Elizabeth Wine
CC30 *Using Part-Time Faculty Effectively,* Michael H. Parsons
CC31 *Teaching the Sciences,* Florence B. Brawer
CC32 *Questioning the Community College Role,* George B. Vaughan
CC33 *Occupational Education Today,* Kathleen F. Arns
CC34 *Women in Community Colleges,* Judith S. Eaton
CC35 *Improving Decision Making,* Mantha Mehallis
CC36 *Marketing the Program,* William A. Keim, Marybelle C. Keim

Contents

Editor's Notes   1
James O. Hammons

Organization development has tremendous potential for the community
college of the future.

Chapter 1. Organization Development: An Overview   5
James O. Hammons

Questions and answers about organization development.

Chapter 2. Organization Development in the Profit Sector: 23
Lessons Learned
Richard W. Woodman
William V. Muse

How can community colleges profit from the experiences of business firms
in implementing organizational development programs?

Chapter 3. Organization Development: 45
Unanswered Questions
Glenn H. Varney

While OD is here to stay, there are still a number of stages before it can be
considered a true profession, says the director of the Management Center
at Bowling Green University and author of a best-selling book on OD.

Chapter 4. The Higher Education Management Institute   55
(HEMI): Organization Development Through Increased
Management Effectiveness
David L. Kest

The west coast director of one of the largest national efforts of an organization development approach to planned change in higher education
describes the project and offers some suggestions for other institutions
interested in institutional change.

Chapter 5. The National Institute: A   69
Partnership for Development
George A. Baker

The director of National Institute for Staff and Organizational Development (NISOD), designed to improve teaching and learning in the community college with an organization development approach, discusses the
results to date.

Chapter 6. Survey Feedback: An Effective OD Intervention   91
Gordon E. Watts

A how-to-do-it discussion of the most widely used and successful OD strategy.

Chapter 7. Organization Development: A President's View   107
Byron N. McClenney

A community college president with ten years of experience, who has also done extensive management consulting, talks about the critical role of the president in managing change.

Chapter 8. Sources and Information Organization   115
Development in the Community College
Anita Colby
James C. Palmer

Additional references on organization development from the ERIC Clearinghouse for Junior Colleges.

Index   131

Editor's Notes

Community colleges are facing some of the greatest challenges in their history. This sourcebook is about organization development, a concept which has vast potential for assisting the people's colleges in meeting these challenges.

The match is perfect. Community colleges, having reached maturity, are now finding it necessary to change and to move in new directions, but to do so with existing staff and few, if any, additional resources. Administrators are finding that strategies for change that were honed to perfection in a growth era are simply fond memories of a bygone day and of little use in a period of curtailment. A new era demands a new strategy, one which recognizes individual needs and goals as well as those of the organization, relies upon planned change, encourages participation by all members of the organization, and encompasses a sufficient variety of techniques to allow a contingency approach to each situation.

Organization development (OD) is that strategy. Much like the modern-day community college, it has grown and evolved. Today it stands ready for use; ideally suited as the change strategy for converting yesterday's community *college* into tomorrow's *community* college.

This volume was written to provide a working understanding of the nature of organization development and of ways in which organization development might be used. The authors have been carefully selected on the basis of their knowledge and experience in organization development and their ability to communicate ideas clearly and succinctly.

The first chapter sets the stage for the entire work. It briefly outlines the origins and history of organization development, describes the steps in implementing the concept, discusses the numerous strategies and interventions used in the planned change strategy of organization development, and concludes by outlining some of the expected results.

The next chapter, by William Muse, Dean of the College of Business at Texas A&M, and Richard Woodman, a faculty member at the same university, reviews the experience of business and industry with organization development and offers some recommendations to avoid reinventing the wheel.

1

Following this, Glenn Varney, a long-time scholar and consultant in OD in both profit and nonprofit operations, discusses several factors leading to the development of organization development and some of the unresolved issues facing the emerging field of OD. Varney illustrates the dramatic forces of change at work in our society today and ways in which changes in society have, in turn, affected the life-styles of workers and their expectations about their work environment. The result is tremendous pressure for rapid change in the workplace. He then shows how the emerging field of organization development, while offering significant promise for helping institutions make the necessary transitions, is plagued by a number of problems. Most of these relate to the need for OD to become a true profession, with its own certification procedures and theoretical foundations.

The Higher Education Management Institute (HEMI) may not be the first, but it is certainly the largest, national program designed to use an OD approach to change in higher education institutions. In Chapter Four David Kest, director of the western office of HEMI, traces the development of the HEMI model, outlines its major elements, and discusses the results to date.

Lessons learned by HEMI that are of general use to institutions and OD practitioners include the need to recognize the unique aspects of what appear to be similar institutions with regard to structuring, training, and intervention strategies; the critical nature of governing board involvement in large-scale change efforts; the importance of management development and training and their connection with institutional mission and goals; and the failure of most institutions to address institutional renewal in a systematic manner.

Reflecting the current interest in systematic planned change, the W. K. Kellogg Foundation in 1977 funded the National Institute for Staff and Organizational Development (NISOD), a national project designed to improve teaching and learning in the community college through the use of an external OD agent (NISOD) as a facilitating and motivating force. George Baker, director of the project, describes its implementation strategies, results to date, and future directions. The National Institute for Staff and Organizational Development project, while using an approach very different from HEMI, has demonstrated that significant results can be gained from the assistance of an outside agency in providing information, training, and other on-site assistance to operating colleges.

Specific OD strategies or techniques for causing change include a number of well-developed interventions. Of these, the one which is the most popular and the most effective is survey feedback. Gordon Watts, who is Director of Staff Development at Westark Community College, president-elect of the National Council of Staff, Program and Organizational Development, and a Regional Associate of the Instructional ACCTion Consortium, provides a detailed discussion of the survey feedback approach, including a suggested outline of steps to follow in using it.

Numerous studies have demonstrated repeatedly that the most important person in the community college is the president. To succeed, therefore, any change effort must be understood by and have the support of the president. Bryon McClenney, now in his third term as chief executive officer, this time at the San Antonio Junior College District, offers a perspective on organization development from a management-conscious president.

James O. Hammons
Editor

James O. Hammons is a professor of Higher Education at the University of Arkansas and President of Organization Development Associates.

Some of the most commonly asked questions
about organization development are answered.

Organization Development: An Overview

James O. Hammons

Although this is the first major work on organization development (OD) in the community college, the literature on OD is considerable. The most recent bibliography published by The American Society of Training and Development consists of 110 pages and includes several hundred articles and approximately eighty book entries, over three-fourths of which were written since 1970.

What Is Organization Development?

Until recently, answers to that question would vary, depending upon whom you spoke with or what publication you were reading. Definitions ranged from the view that organization development was designed only to improve human relations, to the opposing view that the focus of OD was upon increasing the effectiveness and efficiency of organizations. You might also have gathered that OD was equated with some particular technique, such as sensitivity training, job enrichment, or participative management. Major reasons for the lack of consensus about OD are the relative newness of the term, the rapid growth of the field of OD, and

J. Hammons (Ed.) *New Directions for Community Colleges: Organization Development—Change Strategies*, no. 37. San Francisco: Jossey-Bass, March 1982.

6

finally, the very broadness of the concept itself. This lack of consensus has created a situation in which virtually any change strategy is called OD.

As experience with the concept has grown, however, an agreement seems to be evolving that OD is a process for beneficial change.

Of all the definitions found in the literature, the one that I prefer is by French and Bell (1978):

> Organization development is a long-range effort to improve an organization's problem-solving and renewal process, particularly through a more effective and collaborative management of organization culture with special emphasis on the culture of formal work teams with the assistance of a change agent, or catalyst, and the use of the theory and technology of applied behavioral science, including action research [p. 14].

The authors go on to elaborate upon several key words or phrases.

Problem-solving process refers to the way an organization faces the opportunities and challenges of its environment (1978, p. 14).

Renewal process is defined by referring to Gordon Lippitt's term "organizational renewal," which he defines as "the process for initiating, creating, and confronting needed changes so as to make it possible for organizations to become or remain viable, to adapt to new conditions, to solve problems, to learn from experiences" (Lippitt, 1960, p. 1).

Culture is the prevailing pattern of activities, interactions, norms, sentiments, beliefs, attitudes, values, and products (1978, p. 14). Culture includes the formal, overt aspects of the organization, such as goals, technology, structure, policies and procedures, products, and financial resources; plus informal, covert aspects such as perceptions, attitudes, feelings, values, informal interactions, and group norms relating to both the formal and informal systems of the organization (1978, p. 16).

Collaborative management of the culture refers to a shared kind of management, not hierarchically imposed (1978, p. 15).

A *work team* is a group composed of subordinates reporting to a superior (1978, p. 16).

A *change agent or catalyst* is a third party, external to the group initiating an OD effort, who may come from within or without the larger organization (1978, p. 16).

Action research is the basic method that is used in most OD efforts. It consists of a preliminary diagnosis, data gathering from the client group, data feedback to the client group, data exploration by the client group, action planning, and action (1978, p. 17).

Is OD Just Another Passing Fad?

A dictionary defines the word "fad" as a practice or interest followed for a time with exaggerated zeal. The community college has seen its share of these: individualized instruction, sensitivity training, management by objectives, program budgeting, zero-based budgeting, Personalized Systems of Institution (P.S.I.), audio-tutorial instruction, and, perhaps, staff development. Varney asks, "Is OD just another passing fad for which managers may wish to get on the bandwagon; or is it a fundamentally new approach to organizational change?" (1977, p. 56).

The question has been one of concern to OD theorists and writers. In 1971 the topic of a symposium by the Organization Development Division of the American Society of Training and Development was "OD: Fad or Fundamental?" (Chase, 1971). It has also appeared as a topic heading in two of the more recent OD books (French and Bell, 1978, p. 262; Varney, 1977, p. 56).

In truth, OD seems to be taking the familiar path of most fads. Certainly, it is being followed with zeal. The literature is mushrooming; conferences and workshops are flourishing; organizations and consultants with OD in their titles are multiplying. But does organization development have enough substance to make a lasting contribution? Varney indicates that "there are many consultants, professors and organizational development specialists associated with the approach who are making OD look like a 'flash in the pan'." He believes the real test of OD will come when a financial crunch hits and institutions have to decide if it's worth keeping. Blake and Mouton, after reviewing several reactions to their article on the topic, conclude that OD is based upon sound propositions and that OD designs that make use of these propositions have the likelihood of producing fundamental change (1971, p. 31).

French and Bell, after careful analysis, conclude that OD will survive for many years to come and that, although current OD technology will be superseded by additional or modified practices in the years ahead, there will always be a need for something like OD (1978, p. 262).

My own belief is that organization development is not destined to be another fad for community colleges to try and then to discard. Rather, it is a major new concept destined to be around for a long time, even though it may not be adopted so quickly or by nearly so many institutions as it will be in business and industry. Hopefully, this will ensure a higher probability of success for those community colleges that do decide to incorporate OD strategies.

What Is the Conceptual Base of Organization Development?

A review of the origins and evolution of OD is useful to anyone seriously interested in the field, as it discloses the tremendous changes that have occurred, and are still occurring, in its development. OD has come a long way from the profession once said to have been described by Harry Levinson as "being in a position similar to the field of medicine 300 years ago when it used leeches as the single treatment for nearly all ailments" (Randall, 1971, p. 1).

OD evolved from the contributions of a number of behavioral scientists and practitioners, many of whom are well known. Two separate but related developments are considered to be the dual trunks of the original OD tree.

The first of these, laboratory training, began in the summer of 1946 when a leadership team consisting of Kurt Lewin, Kenneth Benne, Leland Bradford, and Ronald Lippitt conducted some research and training for community leaders. They discovered that furnishing individual group leaders and groups with data about individual and group behavior stimulated greater interest and appeared to produce more insights and learning than did lectures and seminars (French and Bell, 1978, p. 21). The result was a repeat of the sessions the following year. Later, these summer meetings led to the birth of the National Training Laboratories (now the NTL Institute for Applied Behavior Science) and contemporary in-group training (French and Bell, 1978, p. 21). During the next ten years, as additional workshops were held, the leadership teams noticed that skills learned in the company of strangers in settings away from the workplace were not transferring to the job. In 1957, the late Douglas McGregor, working in collaboration with John Paul Jones, established a small internal consulting group that began to make some progress in overcoming the problems of transferring behavioral skills and insights that individuals acquired in a laboratory setting to the solution of problems in organizations (French and Bell, 1978, p. 21).

Another significant step in the evolution of laboratory training occurred in 1958 and 1959 when Herbert Shephard initiated a series of organization development interventions at ESSO (now EXXON), using laboratory techniques to improve work group functioning at three refineries: Bayonne, Baton Rouge, and Bayway. Joining Shephard at two of the refineries was Robert Blake. They drew the following conclusions:

1. Top management should be actively involved in planning and leading the program.
2. More team development and conflict resolution should occur with fellow workers than among strangers.
3. In-house personnel could be used as consultants to other managers.
4. External consultants and internal staff need to cooperate in organization development.

At Bayway, Blake and Mouton's "instrumented laboratory" was used; it was later developed into the managerial grid approach to organization development. While it is not known who coined the term "organization development," it is generally thought to have come from the work of Blake, Shephard, and Mouton during this time.

The second trunk of the OD tree is known as survey research and feedback, which refers to the use of attitude surveys and data feedback in workshop sessions. This concept was developed at about the same time by staff members at the Survey Research Center (SRC) of the University of Michigan, led by Rensis Likert, who began applying the action research model of Kurt Lewin. As a result of numerous studies during the next several years, refinements were made by the SRC staff in survey methodology. These included administering the same carefully constructed questionnaire to all respondents, the use of rigorous probability samples, and carefully controlled coding procedures, and the techniques of feedback methodology.

How Does OD Differ From Management Development?

Several authors (Burke and Schmidt, 1971; Varney, 1977; and Zenger, 1978) have written about the differences and the similarities between OD and management development. The consensus appears to be that there are differences, but that there should not be. As commonly practiced, management development is oriented toward developing the skills of individuals. It is often initiated when specific problems in management are detected or as part of an institutionalized training program for one or more categories of personnel. Training to correct specific problems usually consists of short, intensive activities. Most often, manager training occurs at off-site locations, where managers attend university seminars, short courses, or workshops designed to teach or improve skills in areas such as problem solving or decision making or to provide information about topics such as job rotation or job enrichment. To become leaders or trainers in these activities, a person needs skills in diagnosing management needs and the ability to design and conduct workshops. Quite commonly, the results of management development are limited to individual change and are not felt by the manager's organization; in fact, managers who use new abilities often find that their skills are not compatible with their organization's norms and practices.

OD is a much broader concept than management development. It focuses on nurturing the ability of the organization (or some subunit) to grow and develop and is initiated when problems in the organization or some subsystem are detected. Typically, OD strategies are implemented on the job, involve one or more work units, and are focused on group-oriented topics such as team building, conflict resolution, or survey feedback, all of which require considerable time to deal with. Successful OD facilitators usually are broadly trained individuals who, in addition to being skilled in various management development topics, are capable of applying planned change strategies in a work situation.

When viewed at their extremes, management development and organization development are markedly different. Ideally, however, they are interrelated and interdependent. The development of an effective program requires the development of those who can manage in the new climate. It does little good to develop managers without changing the work environment so that their newly acquired knowledge and skills have fertile soil in which to grow. As Zenger stated, "Without skillful managers . . . programs are simply frosting looking for a cake" (1978, p. 3).

What Makes OD Different from Other Change Strategies?

This question is asked by administrators who harbor (with justification) a certain degree of skepticism about anything new that promises to improve organizational performance.

Organization development represents change that is planned, is pursued in a systematic fashion, is expected to occur over a long period, is systems-oriented, is managed, is based upon participation and involvement by those concerned, takes into account both data and experience, emphasizes goal setting and planning, is implemented with a contingency approach, and focuses on intact work teams.

Change occurs in every organization. Most changes, especially in educational institutions, could best be described as evolutionary. Blake and Mouton explain that this type of change occurs

> When men are unwilling or unprepared to confront their disagreements. . . . Evolutionary change comes in small adjustments in response to emerging problems within the *status quo* framework. Such small adjustments rarely violate tradition. . . . Underlying these changes is the assumption that progress is possible if each problem is dealt with as it arises. . . . This is problem-solving-as-you-go development. Only problems which force themselves into the focus of attention are dealt with. . . . But evolutionary processes are painfully slow [1970, p. 11].

A second less successful or planned approach to change is revolution, the types of "changes . . . usually championed by men so deeply frustrated that their overwhelming desire is for a speedy change of any kind and the relief that accompanies it after a long period of suffering. . . . Negative side effects usually result" (Blake and Mouton, 1970, p. 11). Fortunately, this approach is rare in higher education.

The organization development approach involves systematic change that relies upon a deliberate assessment of where an organization wants to be, followed by consideration of where it is. A plan is then developed to close the gap. Simple knowledge of the gap does not make change happen; rather, change demands the participation of members of the organization in making things happen that meet the needs and goals of the organization and the individual. Once planned, change is managed to see that events occur according to plan and that required changes are made.

All too often, change strategies and change strategists from inside and outside an organization offer the promise of quick solutions to complex problems. In contrast, changes made through an organization development approach normally require much more time. This is due to two other characteristics of OD change: its systems orientation and its stress upon widespread involvement, both of which require additional time.

> A systems orientation views and emphasizes organizational phenomena and dynamics in their interrelatedness, their connectedness, their interdependence, and their interaction. Issues, events, forces, and incidents are not viewed as isolated phenomena. A systems approach encourages analysis of events in terms of multiple causation rather than single causation. One cannot change one part of a system without influencing other parts in some ways. The final point is that if one wants to change a system, one changes the system, not just its component parts. [French and Bell, 1978, pp. 77–78].

Naturally, this kind of analysis and approach to change takes more time than a quick band-aid approach. More time is also required when an effort is made to obtain participation and involvement. This time is a worthwhile investment because people support what they help create (Beckhard, 1969, p. 27).

The value placed upon data and experience are two other distinguishing characteristics of OD-induced change. OD interventions are designed either to generate data or to plan actions based on data, specifically data about the system itself. As a consequence, organization members learn how to collect, work with, and utilize data. Unlike the data generated in other approaches, OD data are *described*, not *evaluated*—a subtle but important difference. When data are described, the tendency is to become less defensive about them than when they are evaluated. Additionally, in OD programs, data are used as aids to problem solving, not as ammunition to punish people. This reliance on member involvement in gathering and interpreting data soon leads to making decisions on a factual basis rather than on a basis of power, position, tradition, or persuasion (French and Bell, 1978, pp. 78–80).

The OD approach to change relies upon experience and a belief that people learn through practice. Instead of treating hypothetical problems and abstract organizational issues, OD strategies emphasize the real behavior of individuals and groups and real problems (French and Bell, 1978, p. 80).

Other characteristics of the OD approach are the stress on goal setting and planning and the insistence that these activities be carried out at the individual, group, and organizational levels rather than solely in the top echelons of the organizations. Numerous OD interventions concentrate on developing goal- and objective-setting skills and on developing strategies for achieving them. In selecting interventions, a contingency approach is employed whereby each situation determines the specific intervention(s) used. "In OD *how* things are done is as important as *what* is done; that is, the process of the OD program—how it is done—is as important as the *content* of the OD program—what is done" (French and Bell, 1978, p. 70).

Finally, organization development effects change within intact organizational units, rather than through individual participation in off-campus "stranger-type" training sessions. This is due to the belief that significantly greater and more lasting returns in effectiveness come from intact work teams.

**What Should Be the Outcomes
of a Successful OD Program?**

The results of an OD will depend largely upon the objectives initially established for the program. The following is a composite of typical objectives found in the literature (Bennis, 1969; Beckhard, 1969; Blake and Mouton, 1970).

- creating an open problem-solving climate
- supplementing the authority of role and status with the authority of knowledge and competence
- locating decision making and problem solving as close to information sources as possible
- building trust and collaboration among persons and groups throughout an organization
- developing a reward system that recognizes the organizational mission and the growth of people
- helping managers to manage according to relevant objectives, rather than past practices
- increasing self-control and self-direction for people within the organization

- increasing problem-solving capacities
- improving the ability to take in and communicate information reliably and validly
- clarifying goals and objectives
- improving understanding and acceptance of group processes, including decision making and problem solving
- facilitating the exposure and better management of conflict
- making competition more relevant to goals
- increasing the sense of ownership of organization objectives throughout the work force
- integrating individual needs and organizational goals
- expanding receptivity to changes induced by the environment
- dealing with growth and decay
- relating education and training to organizational priorities
- increasing candor between supervisors and subordinates
- helping an organization escape the rigidities of red tape and fixed procedures that hamper sound decision making
- setting high objectives and achieving them
- improving personal competency
- enhancing the effectiveness of work teams
- strengthening working relationships among teams
- increasing respect for the individual
- instituting ways to reward producers
- increasing innovation and experimentation
- facilitating flexibility in leadership to suit the situation
- making decisions on the basis of information rather than organizational roles
- creating an internal climate of support and freedom from threat
- encouraging better planning
- developing a willingness-to-learn attitude

How Effective Is OD in Achieving These Objectives?

Research on OD, as with most of the applied behavioral sciences, lags behind practice, partly because of the difficulties of conducting research on OD and partly because of the emphasis on getting results rather than on collecting research data. Despite these problems, there is a significant body of research literature which, although limited in scope and methodology, is growing steadily.

Thus far, two compilations of research on OD have been made. The first was by Friedlander and Brown in 1974. Their review, based upon 175 sources, was divided into two broad categories: research related to theories of interventions into the technology (task methods and processes) and the structure (the relationships, roles, and arrangements) of the organization, and research aimed at the human participants and the organization process (communication, problem solving, and decision making) through which individual and organization goals are attained. A second review was conducted by Alderfer in 1977. Alderfer, while acknowledging a need for more systematic research, found "the overall quality of research on OD is showing increasing signs of both rigor and vigor" (p. 272). His review encompassed 104 citations. A third review is scheduled to be published soon in the *Annual Review of Psychology*. Both of the published reviews were scholarly efforts to locate and synthesize available research. Both contain enough evidence of successful results from OD interventions to satisfy even the most outspoken critics.

In addition to these two reviews of OD literature, authors of major books on OD have also included research data in their works sections. Typical of these is the book by French and Bell (1978), considered by many to be a classic in the field. Their conclusion, after reviewing the published research to date, is quite simple: "There is considerable evidence to suggest that OD works" (p. 252).

What Are the Steps Involved in Implementing OD?

Organization development varies among organizations and practitioners. OD programs normally proceed in several stages, which are described below.

Stage One: Awareness of the Need for Change. This stage is often called "recognition of the problem." A prerequisite to implementing any change is for managers to perceive that the organization wishes to improve its position or that it is in a state of imbalance due to some problem. Either condition may result from competition, growth, decline, changes in environment, or an internal or external assessment of the organization's performance against future needs; a kind of "where are we and where do we want to be?" analysis.

Stage Two: Diagnosis. The first steps in diagnosis are to examine the strengths and weaknesses of the system, to define the exact problem that needs to be solved, and to identify causal forces in the situation. These steps are customarily taken when the change agent enters the scene. If the person is a member of the organization, he or she is called an internal change agent; if the person is from outside, he or she is an external change agent.

Whether change agents are internal or external, their first priority is to establish a good working relationship with the organization. Such a relationship involves open communication, feelings of trust, and shared responsibility. It is at this stage that matters relating to responsibility, rewards, and objectives are settled.

Part of the diagnosis consists of determining which data are needed. Numerous authors have developed elaborate ways of conceptualizing this process (French and Bell, 1978, pp. 52–60; Harrison, 1970; Blake and Mouton 1968) but we will not review them here. Once the needs are determined, the data are gathered and analyzed. Considerable attention is given to how information is collected and what is done with it (French and Bell, 1978, p. 62).

Stage Three: Action Plans, Strategies, and Techniques. This stage is often referred to as the intervention stage, the point at which something is done about those areas found to be deficient or problematical in stage two. A later section will discuss the extensive array of OD interventions now available to the OD practitioner. The major point to be made here is that the best practitioners usually have carefully developed plans for conducting interventions that are designed to fit the situation and sufficiently flexible to accommodate changes in the situation.

Stage Four: Monitoring, Evaluating, and Stabilizing. Once strategies are implemented, the next steps are to monitor the situation in order to ensure that things go according to plan and that revisions are made if needed; to evaluate in order to determine if the strategy achieved desired results; and, if results are as intended, to stabilize the new behavior so the system will not regress to its former state. Where external change agents are used, this stage also includes assisting the organization to become independent.

Are There Any Prerequisites for Successful OD?

Holding what is clearly a minority view, Schaffer states that positing a list of prerequisites for OD success "confuses cause and effect . . . [These conditions] are likely to be achievable only as the result of a good OD program and not in advance of it." Further, Schaffer contends that advancing an ideal management style as a prerequisite ignores a "mountain of evidence that effective managers employ many different styles and approaches; it also ignores the growing evidence that it isn't possible to force all managers into the same mold, and that it is self-defeating even to try." According to this minority view, imposing a list of prerequisites amounts to putting the cart before the horse; that, for example, requiring managers to specify their objectives first ignores the fact that "managements most in need of organization development are those least able to state their goals . . . and that an OD program should "begin with what the organization's managers are ready, willing, and able to undertake—rather than what they are unable, unwilling, and not ready to tackle" (Schaffer, 1971, p. 23).

The majority view is that there are prerequisites; that to conduct an effective OD effort, certain conditions must exist or be produced in the organization; and that management must be converted into an image of what good management ought to be (Blake and Mouton, 1971). These prerequisites include the following.

- Recognition of the need for change and improvement
- Willingness to change on the part of leaders and members in order to better meet the needs of the organization and individuals
- Openness to new ideas on the part of managers so that members (with proper safeguards for their protection) are willing to contribute to problem solving
- Patience by members and leaders to allow adequate time for the three major phases (diagnosis, intervention, evaluation) of planned, systematic change to occur
- Leadership ability to carry out agreed upon changes
- Commitment by a majority of members, including key influential leaders
- Clarity of goals and objectives of the OD effort
- Support of OD by top-level and unit management to ensure managerial participation and cooperation with most suggested changes
- Facilitative resources within the organization, or sufficient funds to buy them from the outside
- Orientation for leaders and members to ensure their understanding of the OD process
- Awareness of the interdependence of the system and willingness to change related systems if necessary
- Group or team involvement of work groups and team leaders, rather than "stranger" groups

- Sufficient organizational health to ensure survival until the OD program is completed.

What Are the Strategies Used in OD?

These strategies are called interventions, which means "interference." OD deliberately interferes with the ordinary functioning of the organization in order to correct or modify an ineffective operation. The interventions used in OD are changing constantly as practitioners modify existing approaches and devise new methods. This is due to "new blood" in the field, new problems to be solved, and an increasing knowledge base. Numerous authors have attempted to classify OD interventions (Blake and Mouton, 1976; French and Bell, 1978; Harrison, 1970; Schmuck and Miles, 1971). A review of any of these attempts at developing a classification scheme reveals a certain amount of redundancy because some interventions appear in several classification categories and some classification categories overlap considerably. This may be confusing to some, but it represents what actually exists. While interventions can usually be thought of as belonging to one classification category, most can be used in different ways.

With this in mind, a typology of interventions used by French and Bell (1978) is presented below to outline the currently available groups or types of OD interventions.

1. Diagnostic activities: Fact-finding activities designed to ascertain the state of the system, the status of a problem, and the way things are.
2. Team-building activities: Activities designed to enhance the effective operation of system teams.
3. Intergroup activities: Activities designed to improve the effectiveness of interdependent groups.
4. Survey-feedback activities: These center on actively working with the data produced by a survey and designing action plans based on the survey data.
5. Education and training activities: Activities designed to improve the skills, abilities, and knowledge of individuals.
6. Structural interventions: The broad class of interventions or change efforts aimed at improving organization effectiveness through changes in the task, structural, and technological subsystems. Included in these activities are certain forms of job enrichment, management by objectives,

sociotechnical systems, collateral organizations, and physical-settings interventions.

7. Process consultation activities: Activities on the part of the consultant "which help the client to perceive, understand, and act upon process events which occur in the client's environment" (Schein, 1969, p. 9).

8. Grid organization development activities: Activities invented and franchised by Robert Blake and Jane Mouton, which constitute a six-phase change model involving the total organization (Blake and Mouton, 1968).

9. Third-Party Peacemaking Activities: Activities conducted by a skilled consultant (the third party), which are designed to "help two members of an organization manage their interpersonal conflict" (Walton, 1971, p. 1).

10. Coaching and counseling activities: Efforts of the consultant or other organization members to help individuals define learning goals, learn how others see their behavior, and learn new modes of behavior to see if the new behavior helps them to achieve their goals.

11. Life- and career-planning activities: Activities that enable individuals to focus on their life and career objectives and see how they might go about achieving them.

12. Planning and goal-setting activities: Activities that include theory and experience in planning and goal setting, utilizing problem-solving models, planning paradigms, ideal organization versus real organization discrepancy models, and the like.

As shown above, the tools of the trade of organization development encompass a wide variety of activities. In the hands of a skilled OD practitioner, they are powerful instruments for change.

Does Organization Development Work in Higher Education?

While there is admittedly a small data base for the use of organization development in a college setting, the success of two large national projects involving hundreds of colleges does seem to indicate that OD can be implemented successfully in a collegiate environment. (For discussion of these, see the chapters in this sourcebook written by Baker and Kest.)

Must OD Start at the Top?

No, although earlier theorists adopted this position. Experience has demonstrated that OD can be implemented successfully at any level in the organization.

Where Can I Get More Information About OD?

The last section of this book contains a list of materials currently available in the ERIC system related to organization development in the community college. As may be expected, the amount of literature is not extensive. However, a number of excellent bibliographies of the general literature in the field exist, the most comprehensive of which is published by the American Society for Training and Development, Organization Development Division, Suite 305, 600 Maryland Avenue, S.W., Washington, D.C. 20024. Ask for the 1978 Bibliography and the 1980 Supplement.

For those who don't want to order the bibliography but would like one or two major sources to read, I suggest two books:

French, W. L., and Bell, C. H., Jr. *Organization Development: Behavioral Science Interventions for Organization Improvement.* Englewood Cliffs, N.J.: Prentice-Hall, 1978.

Varney, G. H. *Organization Development For Managers.* Reading, Mass.: Addison-Wesley, 1977.

Both books provide a good overview of the field of OD. The Varney book is slightly shorter and is oriented more to the manager than to the OD practitioner. The French and Bell book is a revised version of one of the classics in the field. Both contain ample bibliographies.

References

Alderfer, C. P. "Organization Development." In M. W. Rosenzweig and L. W. Porter (Eds.), *Annual Review of Psychology*, 1978, *28*, 197–223.

Beckhard, R. *Organization Development: Strategies and Models.* Reading, Mass.: Addison-Wesley, 1969.

Bennis, W. G. *Organization Development: Its Nature, Origins, and Prospects.* Reading, Mass.: Addison-Wesley, 1969.

Blake, R. R., and Mouton, J. S. *Consultation.* Reading, Mass.: Addison-Wesley, 1976.

Blake, R. R., and Mouton, J. S. *Corporate Excellence Through Grid Organization Development: A Systems Approach.* Houston: Gulf, 1968.

Blake, R., R., and Mouton, J. S. "OD—Fad or Fundamental?" *Training and Development Journal*, January 1970, pp. 9–17. (Also contained in Chase below.)

21

Burke, W. W., and Schmidt, W. H. "Management and Organization Development: What is the Target of Change?" *Personnel Administrator, V* (I) March/April 1971. Contained in Zawacki, R. A. and Warrick, D. D. *Organization Development: Managing Change in the Public Sector.* Chicago: International Personnel Association, 1976.

Chase, P. H. (Ed.). *OD—Fad or Fundamental* Organization Development Division, American Society of Training and Development, 1971.

French, W. L., and Bell, C. H., Jr. *Organization Development: Behavioral Science Interventions for Organization Improvement.* Englewood Cliffs, N.J.: Prentice-Hall, 1978.

Friedlander, F. and Brown, L. D. "Organization Development." *Annual Review of Psychology,* 1974, *25,* pp. 313-41.

Harrison, R. "Choosing the Depth of Organization Intervention." *Journal of Applied Behavioral Science,* 1970, *6* (2), pp. 180-202.

Lippitt, G. L. *Organization Renewal.* New York: Appleton-Century-Crofts, 1969.

Randall, L. K. "Some Personal Reflections on 'OD—Fad or Fundamental?'" In P. H. Chase (Ed.), *OD—Fad or Fundamental?* Organization Development Division, American Society of Training and Development, 1971.

Schaffer, R. H. "Comments on 'OD—Fad or Fundamental?' " In P. H. Chase (Ed.), *OD—Fad or Fundamental?* Organization Development Division, American Society of Training and Development, 1971.

Schein, E. H. *Process Consultation: Its Role in Organization Development.* Reading, Mass.: Addison-Wesley, 1969.

Schmuck, R. A., and Miles, M. B. (Ed.). *Organization Development in Schools.* Palo Alto, Calif.: National Press Books, 1971.

Varney, G. H. *Organization Development for Managers.* Reading, Mass.: Addison-Wesley, 1977.

Walton, R. D. *Interpersonal Peacemaking Confrontations and Third Party Consultation.* Reading, Mass.: Addison-Wesley, 1971.

Zenger, J. H. "Organization Development and Management Development: Friends or Foes?" Organization Development Division, American Society of Training and Development, 1978.

Hammons is a professor of Higher Education at the University of Arkansas and President of Organization Development Associates.

*How can community colleges profit from the
experiences of business firms in implementing
organizational development programs?*

Organization Development in the Profit Sector: Lessons Learned

Richard W. Woodman
William V. Muse

Just a short time ago only a handful of business firms had much experience with organization development programs. During the 1970s this changed dramatically. Today the vast majority of large and medium-sized corporations have some familiarity with OD. It is not at all uncommon for firms to have some formally designated positions devoted to organization development, usually within the personnel or human resource function. A large number of firms employ OD consultants from outside the organization or desegregate internal people to fulfill that role. Various OD programs are likely to be under way at any time, and OD processes and concepts have permeated much of the activity performed by personnel or human resources staffs. In short, what was once new is not so new anymore. For better or worse, organization development is now an accepted practice in many firms.

So, what has been learned? What sorts of techniques and methodologies are successful at improving work group or organiza-

J. Hammons (Ed.) *New Directions for Community Colleges: Organization Development—Change Strategies,* no. 37. San Francisco: Jossey-Bass, March 1982.

tional effectiveness and under what conditions are they useful? The purpose of this chapter is to provide some answers to these questions. A basic assumption guiding our efforts is that many private sector organizations make greater use of the social technology of organization development than do most community colleges. As community colleges move to incorporate OD, there is no need to reinvent the wheel.

We will begin by looking at the evolution of organization development in industry and some ways in which organizations (and our perceptions of them) are changing. Next, we will review some empirical evaluations of specific intervention methodologies and provide suggestions for their use. Finally, private sector experiences with organization development programs will be discussed with regard to their implications for community colleges.

Evolution and Congruent Trends

Many of the ideas, concepts, and strategies currently used for improving organizations existed long before organization development emerged as a field of applied behavioral science. Indeed, there are trends in the way our society organizes and manages its enterprises that are very consistent with OD precepts and values, (Tannenbaum and Davis, 1969). Organization development has both contributed to and benefited from these trends; in some sense, it may be a natural outgrowth of them. In addition, OD itself has undergone an evolution since its emergence as a distinct field. In particular, there have been shifts from a high reliance on sensitivity training as an intervention method to the use of team development, which provides more focus on the group's or organization's task. In a like manner, organizations have begun to make more effective use of attitude surveys, often employing them within the context of an OD intervention called survey feedback. Additional trends toward a greater use of sociotechnical systems theory to support OD interventions, a greater reliance on more complex (and adaptable) organizational structures, and more comprehensive approaches to designing work will be discussed in turn.

From Sensitivity Training to Team Development

Histories of organization development often recognize laboratory education or laboratory training as one of the major stems or basic sources for the field (French and Bell, 1978; Huse, 1980).

Sensitivity training or training-group methodology has long been a central experience or principal vehicle for learning within the laboratory education tradition (Schein and Bennis, 1965). This training focuses on increasing participants' awareness of their own and others' behavior in the group setting, improving understanding of group processes, and generally increasing individuals' skills in working with others. The focus is highly interpersonal; the agenda is focused on behavior occurring immediately in the group setting. Sensitivity training was a popular intervention methodology during the early days of OD. This popularity, coupled with the large number of interventions having their origin in early laboratory training methodology, has caused the entire field of OD to suffer from an overidentification with the use of T-groups (Strauss, 1976). While this misunderstanding is not as severe today, some problems remain (Woodman, 1980).

Over time, the T-group has proved to be far less effective in the organizational setting—where the focus often must be on work group effectiveness—than it is when the primary concern is increasing individual interpersonal skills. Thus, gradually, the field of OD has shifted away from relying on T-groups as a primary methodology and has concentrated instead on the development of groups and teams with a clearer task focus (Dyer, 1977; French and others, 1978).

Team development or team building has become one of the most commonly used and important organizational change technologies (Beer, 1976). While similar to sensitivity training in its theoretical foundation and concern with the group process, team development focuses more clearly on organizationally relevant issues. Simply stated, the objective of team development is to improve the effectiveness of work groups. The agenda for team development groups is the task; interpersonal issues are generally relevant only to the extent that they affect performance of the group's task.

The shift from sensitivity training to team development is interesting in a larger sense also as it demonstrates the heightened concern of OD practitioners with group and organizational effectiveness. While certain interpersonal variables (such as openness and trust) are likely to remain key targets of change in OD programs, they are increasingly likely to be viewed as instrumental goals rather than as ends in themselves. An effective OD program may result in technical and structural changes as well as in changes in organizational and group processes.

26

From Attitude Surveys to Survey Feedback

Survey feedback is an OD intervention that combines gathering survey data from members of the organization with a process of information sharing and collaborative action planning to effect organizational change (Bowers and Franklin, 1974). Of course, large American corporations have been conducting surveys of employee attitudes for a long time. Indeed, the third phase (conducted from 1928 to 1930) of the famous Hawthorne studies was actually a large-scale attitude survey involving some 21,000 Western Electric employees (Cass and Zimmer, 1975). What is, in effect, an attitude survey is a major component of survey feedback methodology. However, survey feedback differs from the traditional attitude survey along several dimensions—most importantly, in terms of who is involved in the survey and what happens to the data from the survey (French and Bell, 1978). Early attitude surveys typically collected data from employees. This data was then given to management, who used it as a decision-making tool. Surveys done within the context of OD interventions usually collect information at many hierarchical levels in the organization. This information is typically shared with all who participated in the survey, and the responsibilities for corrective actions based upon these data are likewise widely shared. There is considerable evidence that data-based methods such as survey feedback provide a powerful impetus for organizational change (Nadler, 1977). Survey feedback will be described in some detail in chapter six.

From Mechanistic Systems to Sociotechnical Systems

One of the clearer trends in the organizational sciences has been the increasing use of systems models to conceptualize organizations (Katz and Kahn, 1978). Sociotechnical systems theory regards the organization as more than just a technical system for getting things done. In the final analysis, the organization is a collection of human beings—a social system. Changes made in the technical system ultimately impact the social fabric of the organization; thus, for organizational change to be managed effectively, both the social and technical aspects of that change must be dealt with.

Early models of organizations as well as many earlier approaches to organizational change tended to take a more mechanistic view of the organization; that is, the organization was conceptualized in static, rather than dynamic terms and change programs tended to focus thinking and planning on narrow changes in some specific aspect of the organization. However, research and experience has demonstrated time and time again that organizations are both social and technical systems; changes made in one system without adequate concern for their impact on the other are likely to fail at a rate higher than expected (Herbst, 1974; Rice, 1958; Trist, 1969).

Of course, sociotechnical systems theory and research exists in its own right apart from the field of OD. The concept of sociotechnical systems has, however, strongly influenced organization development theory and practice. Indeed, Huse (1980) lists sociotechnical systems theory, along with laboratory training and survey research/feedback, as the three major historical stems of OD. A large class of OD interventions has been developed based upon sociotechnical systems theory.

> The objective [of these interventions] is to optimize the relationship between the social or human systems of the organization and the technology used by the organization to produce output. When these systems are arranged optimally, the organization runs more smoothly than when they are not; output is higher, employees' needs are satisfied better, and the organization remains adaptable to change [Pasmore and Sherwood, 1978, p. 3].

From Static Organizational Forms to Matrix

Not only have models of organizations been changing toward greater complexity, but business organizations themselves have become increasingly complex, requiring new forms of organization. Particularly critical has been the need for structures that would be more flexible and adaptive than the traditional bureaucracy with its rigid hierarchy and standardized procedures.

A form of organization known as "matrix" has been steadily gaining in popularity during the past twenty to thirty years. A matrix may be defined as any organization that employs a multiple-command system (Davis and Lawrence, 1977). This means that the traditional concept of one person-one boss is no longer the rule. In the matrix organization an employee may have two (or more) bosses; for example, a subordinate may report to both a line manager and a functional head. A petroleum engineer in a district production office might be responsible to both the head of petroleum engineering at corporate headquarters and the chief of production operations for the district. Matrices are characterized by decentralized decision making and the extensive use of temporary task forces and teams.

An interesting symbiotic relationship exists between the matrix form of organization and the increased use of organization development programs. For one thing, the matrix helps to create a climate that is both supportive of and receptive to organizational improvement efforts. In a like manner, many features of an OD program, such as an emphasis on collaborative behavior and the effective use of groups and teams, are also important cornerstones for implementing a matrix structure.

There are other examples of organizational forms that can become an integral part (or outcome) of an OD intervention. A promising concept in this vein is the "collateral organization" (Zand, 1974). As a change strategy, collateral organization means the creation of a supplemental organization which coexists with the formal structure. The collateral organization is designed to utilize the groups of people outside the normal communication/authority channels to solve problems facing the system. A collateral organization might be used to gather information during a change effort or to bring expertise to bear on some issue that the formal organization seems unable or unwilling to resolve.

Many structural and work design changes in organizations are increasingly congruent with organization development values and concepts, and OD interventions have often been useful in facilitating transitions to these more effective designs. For example, OD interventions have been used successfully to facilitate an organizational change to a matrix form (Tolchinsky and Woodman, 1981).

From One-Dimensional Job Design
to More Complex Perspectives

Concern with the design of work is certainly not new. What is new, however, is that we have come to view the relationships among the design of the job, the unique psychological makeup of each individual, and the performance of that individual in different and perhaps more insightful ways.

During most of the Industrial Revolution the major impetus for job design came from the movement toward greater and greater task and job specialization. This concern for increased specialization reached its peak with scientific management. The central concepts of scientific management were an attempt to improve effectiveness and productivity through increased task specialization, an identification of the best way to perform each aspect of the work, and an emphasis on standardized performance of this best way once it had been determined. However, changes in our society and the role work plays in our lives forced a greater concern for the individual's social role in organizations. Because of this, there was a continual stream of job design strategies that supposedly were more considerate of the individual. These newer strategies are perhaps epitomized by the concept of job enrichment.

Job enrichment as a job design technique may be described as building into the job greater responsibility, more autonomy, and increased control over the work. As such, it is compatible with the values and goals of OD efforts. However, job enrichment, as it is often practiced, is as one-dimensional as scientific management. A major weakness in traditional job enrichment occurs when management assumes that all employees want enriched work. In reality, there is a wide variance among people not only in terms of their own personalities, attitudes, and values, but also in terms of what they want from their participation in an organization; individuals respond differently to the content of their jobs. The most successful job design programs have recognized this variance.

In order to maximize the motivating potential of jobs, there must be a complex fit among the individual, the job, and the organizational structure/climate (Porter and others, 1975, p. 309). Organization development programs can play an important role in discovering and designing this fit. Indeed, the redesign of jobs is often an important part of a comprehensive organization development program. The design of work represents another area where the evolution of ideas and practice is becoming increasingly compatible with OD principles and precepts.

Empirical Results of OD Interventions

This section examines a number of change strategies that are commonly (although not exclusively) used in organization development programs in industry and looks at the results they have achieved. The purpose of this examination is to develop an understanding of the probable effects of the intervention as well as the context for appropriate use.

There are at least three reasons an organization development program might be ineffective in any given instance: The program just isn't any good (it is ineffective because it simply doesn't work), a potentially effective program is conducted poorly, or a potentially effective program is applied inappropriately (the intervention does not really deal with the problem at hand). These reasons demonstrate the need for a rigorous evaluation of organizational change programs in order to learn from mistakes. The second reason suggests the need for adequate training and knowledge on the part of OD practitioners. The third reason deals with the issue of accurate diagnosis of an organization's problems. This diagnosis is fundamental to an effective change program (Bowers, 1976). Knowledge concerning the current state of affairs is a logical antecedent to planning the change effort as well as evaluating the results of this effort; indeed, learning about the organization is so essential to OD that a whole family of diagnostic interventions has been developed to aid in this regard (Beer, 1980, pp. 111–132). For example, survey feedback is often used as a diagnostic tool.

Even if information concerning an organization can be collected in a reliable and valid manner and the information is used in an accurate identification or diagnosis of problems, the issue of linking this diagnosis with action still remains. Some framework is needed to link problems with specific intervention methodologies designed to deal with those problems in ways appropriate to the particular organization. This linkage has often been recognized as a critical element in the success or failure of an OD effort.

> For constructive organizational change to occur, there must exist an appropriate correspondence of the treatment (action, intervention) with the internal structure and functional conditions of the organization for which change is intended. Since by definition these internal conditions preexist, this means that treatments must be selected, designed, and varied to fit the properties of the organization [Bowers and others, 1975, p. 393].

Specifically with regard to linking the diagnosis with further intervention activities, what sort of framework exists for making these decisions? If the diagnosis reveals X, does this mean the organization should always do A? Experience from industry reveals that a reasonable middle position should be sought between an extreme contingency approach where every situation is regarded as unique and a prescriptive approach based on rigid guidelines. A number of OD writers have proposed models or frameworks for matching interventions with problems revealed by an organizational diagnosis (Blake and Mouton, 1976; Bowers and others, 1975; White and Mitchell, 1976). These models will not be reviewed here; however, a good starting point for applying them comes from an understanding of the probable effects of various change programs. A framework for analyzing these effects is presented below.

Subsystem Effects of Organization Development Interventions

Six major families or classes of organizational change strategies are listed in Table 1: process consultation, team development, survey feedback, sociotechnical, structural interventions, and job redesign. This list is not intended to be exhaustive, nor are the categories mutually exclusive. In fact, a comprehensive OD program may contain many of these activities. For example, the OD program at General Motors combines the application of sociotechnical design concepts, the use of survey feedback, and the utilization of collateral or parallel organizational forms (Miller, 1978a; 1978b; 1978c). Further, the activities are sometimes mixed together so as to be almost inseparable. For example, team development, which usually follows an action research model of data gathering, feedback, and action planning, often contains elements of survey feedback; an action plan based on survey feedback data may be to redesign some jobs; and so on.

In order to isolate possible effects, we conceptualize the organization as an open system composed of four major subsystems that are identified by their related concepts or constructs as follows:

- a work flow subsystem—task, technology
- a social subsystem—interpersonal relationships, informal groups, norms, organizational climate/culture
- a managerial/control/information subsystem—rules, procedures, policies, personnel information systems, management information systems
- an organizational/group structure subsystem—communication/authority relationships, roles, organizational design.

One assumption is that a change in one subsystem ultimately affects all parts of the organization. Thus, while an intervention may be targeted at one aspect of the organization it has a potential impact on the whole (see Figure 1). The list of change strategies in Table 1 are, by definition, organization-wide efforts. The second column of

32

Table 1. Subsystem Effects of
Organization Development Interventions

Organizational Change Strategies	Initial Subsystem Impact	Area of Expected Change
Process Consultation	Social	*Process Variables* (attitudes, values, satisfaction with interpersonal relations, interpersonal skills)
Team Development	Social	(primarily) *Process Variables* (participation and involvement, attitudes, group decision-making and problem-solving skills, organizational climate, satisfaction, possible group effectiveness)
Survey Feedback	Social	*Process Variables* (attitudes, perceptions of the need for change, commitment to change, involvement, organizational climate)
Sociotechnical	Work flow; Social	(primarily) *Outcome Variables* (productivity, performance, absenteeism, turnover, job satisfaction, employee morale)
Structural Change	Organization/group structure; Social	*Process and Outcome Variables* (productivity, performance, communications, decision making, organizational climate)
Job Redesign	Work flow	(primarily) *Outcome Variables* (productivity, job satisfaction, quality of production, motivation, involvement, absenteeism, turnover)

Table 1 indicates which subsystem(s) is initially changed by the intervention.

When measuring the impact of change programs, it is often useful to draw a distinction between process variables and outcome variables (Porras and Berg, 1978). Process variables are such things as attitudes, decision-making and problem-solving skills, group processes, motivation, involvement, openness, trust, and communication skills. Examples of outcome variables are performance level, effectiveness, efficiency, productivity, absenteeism, turnover, and job satisfaction. While many of these variables are naturally related, and results are sometimes equivocal, there does seem to be a tendency for different types or classes of interventions to have their

Figure 1. System Effects of Organization Development Programs

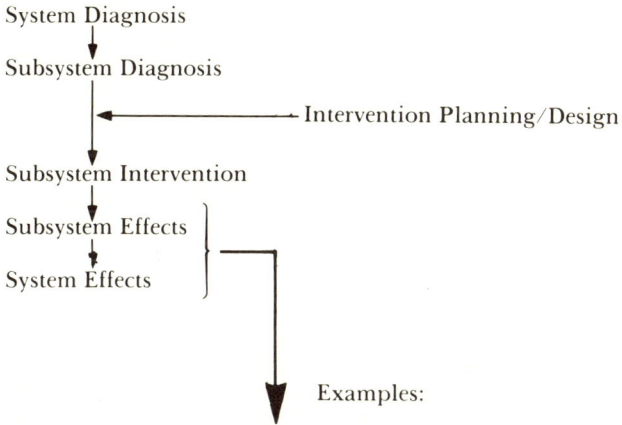

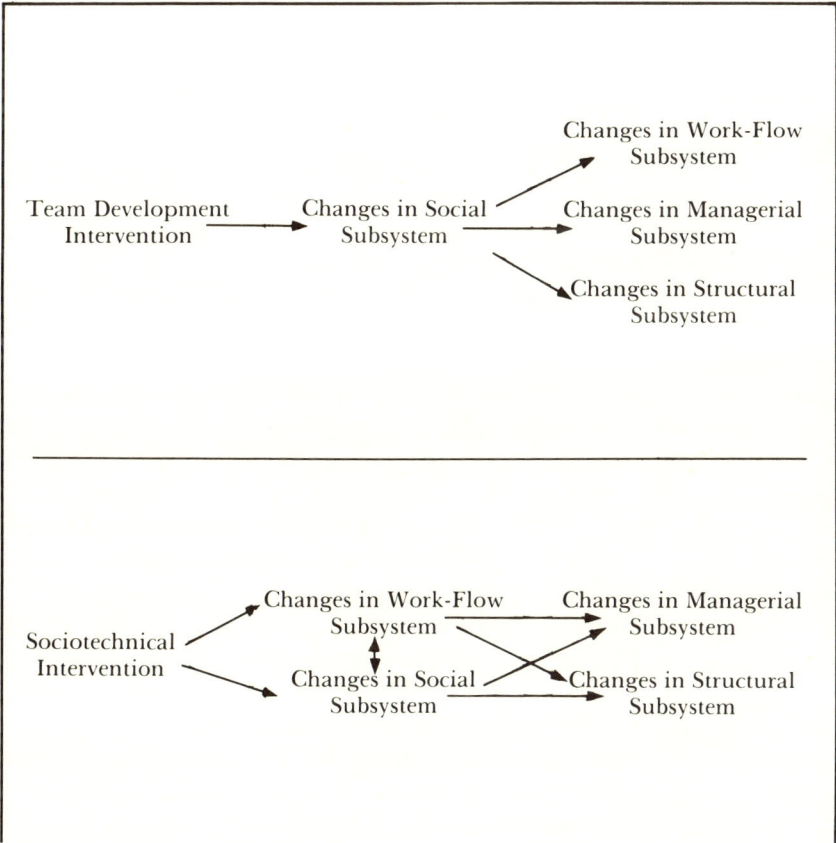

System Diagnosis

Subsystem Diagnosis

Intervention Planning/Design

Subsystem Intervention

Subsystem Effects

System Effects

Examples:

Team Development Intervention → Changes in Social Subsystem →
- Changes in Work-Flow Subsystem
- Changes in Managerial Subsystem
- Changes in Structural Subsystem

Sociotechnical Intervention →
- Changes in Work-Flow Subsystem
- Changes in Social Subsystem

Changes in Managerial Subsystem

Changes in Structural Subsystem

initial impact in either process or outcome areas. This expected initial change is indicated in the third column of Table 1.

Each of these six major change strategies will be described in general terms below along with some results from private sector corporate experience with their use.

Process Consultation. Process consultation may be defined as ". . . a set of activities on the part of the consultant which help the client to perceive, understand, and act upon process events which occur in the client's environment" (Schein, 1969, p. 9). Process consultation focuses on improving interpersonal and group processes and is characterized by the use of a skilled third party, although the process consultant need not be an outsider to the organization. Process consultation has been selected as an example of interventions that focus on process concerns or a concern with individual and group work styles. Other interventions that might be included in this category are sensitivity training, third-party interventions that focus specifically on interpersonal conflict (Walton, 1969), and some forms of team development.

Schein (1969) argued that process consultation is designed to change some attitudes and values held by members of the organization and to increase interpersonal skills. Ultimately increased performance is expected to be related to these changes in values and skills, although in the short run an evaluator should look for evidence that values are changing or skills are increasing. In their review of the OD research literature, Friedlander and Brown (1974) conclude that process approaches have positive effects on the attitudes of participants, but that there is no evidence for increased performance or effectiveness following processual interventions. Kaplan (1979b), in his review of the research literature specifically devoted to process consultation, reaches a similar conclusion: No studies exist that support the view that process consultation promotes task effectiveness. On the other hand, several controlled laboratory experiments have provided support for anticipated changes in process variables following a process consultation intervention. For example, Lipshitz and Sherwood (1978) report higher levels of cohesiveness and improved work processes in task groups receiving a process intervention when compared to control groups. However, there were no actual performance differences between treatment and control groups. In a similar vein, Kaplan (1979a) reports greater involvement and satisfaction with interpersonal relationships following process consultation. Again, actual group performance was not improved.

Using the conceptual scheme presented here, we can conclude that process consultation interventions initially affect—and are, in fact, designed to affect—the social subsystem of the organization. Experience from business indicates that changes in numerous process variables (see Table 1 for examples) are likely following a well-done process consultation effort. Measurable changes in other subsystems of the organization are problematic and probably should not be expected. However, note that possible changes in outcome variables would have been extremely difficult to detect in many reported studies done in business organizations due to severe methodological constraints. Often actual performance was not measured or was measured inadequately. Also, many studies failed to isolate the impact of process consultation from other activities of a change program (Kaplan, 1979b). Indeed, process consultation activities permeate much of the change efforts in OD and, in reality, process consultation seldom is performed by itself.

Team Development. There are several different models or variations of interventions that fall under the label of team development. These vary from an initial focus on interpersonal and group process issues to an emphasis on goal setting, action planning, and problem solving (Beer, 1976). Regardless of the form that team building takes, all models generally follow the action research process and emphasize group participation, the discovery and confrontation of problems facing the work group, and planning for ways to overcome these problems. The ultimate goal, again regardless of differences in focus, is the creation of healthy work groups that are capable of recognizing barriers to effective functioning and designing and implementing strategies to remove these barriers.

Friedlander and Brown (1974) concluded that team development activities often affect participant attitudes and sometimes affect their behavior as well. That conclusion is also generally supported by a comprehensive literature review focusing specifically on team development research (Woodman and Sherwood, 1980b). There is considerable empirical support for the idea that team development can result in a variety of positive outcomes for groups and organizations, and many authors consider team building to be one of the more powerful and well-developed OD techniques (Alderfer, 1977; Beer, 1976). However, team development suffers, as does process consultation, from a lack of hard evidence that links it conclusively with improved group or organizational effectiveness. There is a higher probability, in any given instance, that improvement resulting from team building is more likely to manifest itself in changes in process variables than in changes in outcome variables. On a more positive note there is fairly strong evidence for many of the expected changes shown in Table 1. (See Woodman and Sherwood, 1980b, for a review of studies reporting these results.) Among the strongest expected outcomes of a team development intervention is an increase in the amount of involvement and participation in the group (Friedlander, 1967; Woodman and Sherwood, 1980a). This may be a particularly valuable result since organization development practitioners attach great value to collaborative behavior and often assume that widespread participation is necessary to effect and sustain meaningful changes in the organization.

In general, team development is designed to influence the social subsystem of the firm. In addition, one form of team development focuses on roles of participants in its attempt to improve group functioning (Harrison, 1972). To the extent that the team building focuses on role renegotiation rather than simply role clarification, some initial impacts may be felt in the structural subsystem as it is defined here.

Survey Feedback. As previously described, survey feedback consists of the process whereby data are collected (generally by questionnaire) from members of an organization or work group, organized in some meaningful fashion, and fed back to the people who generated the data. Some or all of the participants then use this information as a basis for action planning to deal with identified issues. Huse (1980) suggests that if widespread use is any indication of success, then many organizations have apparently judged survey feedback to be effective, since the volume of usage of this OD technique is so high. Since survey feedback is so often involved as a routine part of many OD programs, as well as being used by itself, it may well be the single most frequently used methodology. Among techniques that are designed to influence directly the social subsystem of the organization, it may often be the most effective. In a well-known study, Bowers (1973) compared the results of survey feedback with several varieties of laboratory education and process consultation interventions in twenty-three organizations. Survey feedback was judged the most effective of the four approaches examined and was the only intervention consistently associated with positive changes in organizational climate.

In general, the research literature suggests that the primary effects of survey feedback will be on participant attitudes and perceptions. There is little evidence that survey feedback, particularly when used alone, will result in changes in organizational effectiveness or performance (Beer, 1976; Friedlander and Brown, 1974). However, survey feedback is often an effective way to provide a critical link in the OD process between diagnosis and action planning. As indicated in Table 1, survey feedback initially affects the social subsystem and its impact should be seen primarily in changes in process variables.

Sociotechnical Interventions. As mentioned previously, sociotechnical interventions focus simultaneously on changing both technical and social aspects of the system in ways designed to optimize their relationship and thus to increase organizational effectiveness. The major impetus for sociotechnical work restructuring efforts came from the Tavistock Institute in England, and for a long time most sociotechnical improvement efforts took place in Europe. During the past decade, however, sociotechnical approaches have been used extensively in the United States to design, build, and manage new plants. Huse (1980) reported that General Foods, General Motors, Proctor and Gamble, PPG Industries, Sherwin-Williams, Cummins Engine, Mead Corporation, H. K. Heinz, Dana Corporation, TRW, Rockwell, and Shell Canada, Ltd., as well as a number of smaller firms, have recently built new facilities utilizing sociotechnical concepts. After exploring this trend, Huse concluded: "At this stage, no one knows how many organizations have initiated new-design (sociotechnical) plants, nor how many actually exist; a guess is that at least 25 large organizations have at least one, and that more than 100 currently in operation, e.g., General Motors has built about 20" (1980, p. 249).

Friedlander and Brown (1974) reported that research studies consistently indicate performance and productivity increases attributable to sociotechnical change programs. Some evidence of impacts on process variables (such as employee morale) exists also. For example, Shell United Kingdom has a successful organization-wide sociotechnical change program that emphasizes both quality of work life and productivity improvements (Hill, 1972). However, the greatest appeal to most business organizations seems to come from the potential impact on group and organizational performance stemming from sociotechnical change strategies. Pasmore and King (1978) compared the effects of sociotechnical systems, job redesign, and survey feedback interventions during a two and one-half year study in a food processing plant. The three interventions had similar positive effects on worker attitudes; however, only the sociotechnical intervention resulted in productivity improvements and cost savings. Sociotechnical change programs are designed to affect both the work flow and the social subsystems, with their major (but not their only) impact being on outcome variables.

Structural Changes. Alderfer (1977) argued that efforts to alter structural properties of organizations have become much more common in OD as interventions have been made into larger and more complex systems. General Motors has been using a permanent collateral organization, which they refer to as a parallel organizational structure, in their Central Foundry Division since 1974 (Miller, 1978b). The administrators of the division established the parallel organization when they became convinced that a more traditional structure was not allowing them to work together effectively. Stein and Kanter (1980) described the successful use of a parallel organization in a firm manufacturing high-technology electric equipment. Further, based on their experiences, Stein and Kanter suggest that parallel organizational forms may be a significant answer to problems facing organizations in the coming decades. One of the major advantages of the parallel organization is that it can function side-by-side with bureaucracy, thus allowing the firm to successfully use the efficiencies represented by bureaucratic structures and perhaps avoid some of the shortcomings (Stein and Kanter, 1980).

The expected improvements stemming from structural change are not particularly well documented. Luke and others (1973) introduced a major structural change into a large retail food chain and reported improvements in attitudes, climate, productivity, and profit. Intererestingly, Luke and others used a team development intervention to facilitate the transition to the new organizational form. This transition is similar to what occurs when team building has facilitated the transition to matrix (Tolchinsky and Woodman, 1981).

In general, structural change initially affects both the organization/group structure subsystem and the social subsystem. Change is likely to be observed in both outcome and process variables, although structural changes are probably undertaken primarily for their anticipated effect on group or organizational performance. The impact of structural change on the organization can be extremely complex, however. For example, research by Nadler and others (1980) indicates that control systems, tasks, and individual differences may moderate the effects of structural change on organizational or subunit performance.

Job Redesign. Job redesign represents a deliberate, planned restructuring of the way work is performed in order to increase workers' motivation, involvement, and efficiency—and hence to improve their performance. As an organizational change strategy, job redesign represents a whole family of specific techniques, including work simplification, job rotation, job enlargement, and job enrichment (Woodman and Sherwood, 1977). Under certain circumstances each of these techniques can be effective in improving work performance in the organization.

The literature is full of reports of favorable results stemming from job design programs (Davis and Cherns, 1975; Davis and Taylor, 1979). One of the most impressive records in this regard was compiled at AT&T, where seventeen of eighteen controlled job design studies had positive results (Ford, 1973). It is also true, however, that the literature contains many examples of failed job redesign programs (Lawler, and others, 1973). Redesign efforts have often ignored individual differences, technological differences, task differences, contextual differences, and so on. In other words, the approach has suffered some from an overgeneralization in applying specific job redesign strategies and a corresponding lack of appreciation for the necessity to refine approaches to better fit the situation and personalities involved. Nevertheless, the tremendous body of theory, research, and practice in this area had produced one of our most powerful and popular organizational change methodologies. Job redesign programs can be expected to have initial impacts on the work flow subsystem, and, if the change program is appropriately designed and managed, changes should manifest themselves primarily in outcome variables.

At some level of abstraction most organizational change programs have an identical goal, and that is to increase system effectiveness. What represents effectiveness is, in a real sense, situation-specific. In the most general terms effectiveness translates into goal accomplishment by an organization or group. However, there are, for a complex system, an infinite, or at least a very large number, of paths to the goal. Certainly, within the field of organization development, a variety of strategies have evolved. While they may share the same ultimate objectives, the various approaches do not work through the system via identical paths, nor should measurable changes be expected to appear in the same kinds of variables. Thus, it is important to understand the strengths, weaknesses, and likely impacts of various change strategies so that intelligent choices can be made by an organization's management regarding the feasibility and appropriateness of any particular OD technology.

Implications for Community Colleges

How can community colleges profit from the experience of business firms in implementing organization development programs? While any OD application must be appropriate for the environment in which it is used, there would appear to be some implications from the industrial experience for community colleges. Any community college administrator planning to implement one or more organizational development techniques would do well to review the results from industry and to select the intervention to be used with some degree of knowledge as to its appropriate application, initial impact, and area of expected change.

The movement from a focus on individual behavior (such as the use of sensitivity training) to more task orientation and team development in industry seems to signal a similar direction for community colleges. While properly structured sensitivity training may still be useful in helping individuals gain greater awareness and understanding of their own behavior and attitudes, greater progress might be made by focusing the efforts of a group on a task in which all members are engaged and for which there is some shared responsibility (such as in team development). It is important that the task be something over which the group has control and that there be a shared concern for improved effectiveness. A group of department or division heads assigned to make recommendations for improvements in the counseling system for helping new students to select majors or areas of study is a task that meets these criteria.

The technique of survey feedback also offers considerable potential for community colleges. Taking a survey of attitudes toward an issue within a unit (a department or division) and sharing the results with the members of that unit could provide the focus for identifying problems and possible solutions to them. Such an approach might be particularly useful in defining and clarifying goals for a department, division, or college. The Institutional Goals Inventory (IGI) instrument developed by the Educational Testing Service is an example of a questionnaire that has been used to survey those involved in an educational institution and to share feedback for purposes of goal setting and planning.

The convincing results on performance in industry from sociotechnical interventions suggest that community college administrators need to be aware of the social dimension to any attempts to modify or change work flow processes. For example, a change in the registration procedure may affect the social/behavioral processes of students, faculty and staff. When combined with other OD approaches such as survey feedback and team development, such sociotechnical interventions may have very positive results in both process and outcomes.

The industrial research on job enrichment has some interesting implications for administrators in terms of job assignment. In many respects, the job of the classroom teacher offers the ultimate in job enrichment opportunities, for the teacher has considerable latitude in the use of teaching methodologies. In short, each teacher has his or her own style, approach, or favored techniques to get the job done. The research in industry suggests that some teachers may find this freedom attractive, while others might prefer a more highly-structured task: standardized and detailed course outlines, preprepared visual aid packages, common exams, etc. An enlightened administrator might provide teachers with a choice.

Tailoring the task to an individual's needs might also be possible. For example, some faculty members might have a strong need for close interpersonal relations with students and, hence, be assigned smaller classes coupled with considerable individual counseling. Other faculty members may dislike close relationships and instead prefer to perform before an audience; they might be assigned large classes with little, if any, individual counseling. All of this suggests that a sensitivity by administrators to the needs of an employee for autonomy versus structure and for interpersonal contact in making job assignments might greatly improve job satisfaction.

As in industry, it is important that OD techniques not be used simply as a means to involve people. The groups involved— students, faulty, administrators, professional staff, etc.—should have an ability to shape and influence the outcome or decision in the area of involvement. And the issues addressed should be important, relevant, and within the scope of individual control. For example, the users of a facility to be constructed, such as a classroom building, should logically be involved in the design of the space they will utilize. Yet the opportunity for involvement should not be offered unless there is a willingness to consider the suggestions made. The suggestions presented may be unfeasible for economic, architectural, or political reasons; feedback about this problem is better than ignoring the suggestion altogether.

The experience in industry suggests that the use of organization development techniques can have very positive results on attitudes, motivation, involvement, and other process variables. Evidence as to OD's impact on outcome variables such as performance and productivity is less convincing but yet also positive for some approaches. However, since the measurement of outcomes in higher education is often elusive, the positive results on process variables would seem to be ample justification for the use of OD techniques in community colleges.

References

Alderfer, C. P. "Organization Development." In M. R. Rosenzweig and L. W. Porter, (Eds.), *Annual Review of Psychology*, 1977, *28*, 197-223.

Beer, M. *Organization Change and Development: A Systems View*. Santa Monica, Calif.: Goodyear, 1980.

Beer, M. "The Technology of Organization Development." In M. D. Dunette (Ed.), *Handbook of Industrial and Organizational Psychology*. Chicago: Rand McNally, 1976. 937-993.

Blake, R. R., and Mouton, J. S. *Consultation*. Reading, Mass.: Addison-Wesley, 1976.

Bowers, D. G. "OD Techniques and Their Results in 23 Organizations: The Michigan ICL Study." *Journal of Applied Behavioral Science*, 1973, *9*, 21-43.

Bowers, D. G. "Organizational Development: Promises, Performances, Possibilities." *Organizational Dynamics*, 1976, *4* (4), 50-62.

Bowers, D. G., Franklin, J. L., and Pecorella, P. A. "Matching Problems, Precursors, and Interventions in OD: A Systemic Approach." *Journal of Applied Behavioral Science*, 1975, *11*, 391-409.

Bowers, D. G., and Franklin, J. L., "Basic Concepts of Survey Feedback." In J. W. Pfeiffer and J. E. Jones (Eds.), *The 1974 Annual Handbook for Group Facilitators*. La Jolla, Calif.: University Associates, 1974.

Cass, E. L., and Zimmer, F. G. (Eds.), *Man and Work in Society*. New York: Van Nostrand Reinhold, 1975.

Davis, L. E., and Cherns, A. B. (Eds.). *The Quality of Working Life* (vols. I and II). New York: Free Press, 1975.

Davis, L. E. and Taylor, J. C. (Eds.). *Design of Jobs*, 2nd ed. Santa Monica, Calif.: Goodyear, 1979.

Davis, S. M., and Lawrence, P. R. *Matrix*. Reading, Mass.: Addison-Wesley, 1977.

Dyer, W. G. *Team Building: Issues and Alternatives*. Reading, Mass.: Addison-Wesley, 1977.

Ford, R. N. "Job Enrichment Lessons from AT&T." *Harvard Business Review*, 1973, *51* (1), 96-106.

43

French, W. L., and Bell, C. H. *Organization Development: Behavioral Science Interventions for Organization Improvement*, (2nd ed.) Englewood Cliffs, N.J.: Prentice-Hall, 1978.

French, W. L., and Bell, C. H., and Zawacki, R. a. *Organization Development: Theory, Practice, and Research*. Dallas: BPI, 1978.

Friedlander, R. "The Impact of Organizational Training Laboratories Upon the Effectiveness and Interaction of Ongoing Work Groups." *Personnel Psychology*, 1967, *20*, 289–307.

Friedlander, R., and Brown, L. D. "Organization Development." In M. R. Rosenzweig and L. W. Porter (Eds.), *Annual Review of Psychology*, 1974, *25*, 313–41.

Harrison, R. "Role Negotiation: A Tough-Minded Approach to Team Development." In W.W. Burke and H. A. Hornstein (Eds.), *The Social Technology of Organization Development*. Fairfax, Va.: NTL, 1972. 84-96.

Herbst, R. G. *Socio-technical Design*. London: Tavistock, 1974.

Hill, P. *Towards a New Philosophy of Management*. New York: Harper and Row, 1972.

Huse, E. F. *Organization Development and Change*. (2nd. ed.) St. Paul, Minn.: West, 1980.

Kaplan, R. E. "The Utility of Maintaining Relationships Openly: An Experimental Study." *Journal of Applied Behavioral Science*, 1979a, *15*, 41–59.

Kaplan, R. E. "The Conspicuous Absence of Evidence That Process Consultation Enhances Task Performance." *Journal of Applied Behavioral Science*, 1979b, *15*, 346–60.

Katz, D., and Kahn, R. L. *The Social Psychology of Organizations*, 2nd ed. New York: Wiley, 1978.

Lawler, E. E., Hackman, F. R., and Kaufman, S. "Effects of Job Redesign: A Field Experiment." *Journal of Applied Social Psychology*, 1973, *3*, 49–62.

Lipshitz, R., and Sherwood, J. J. "The Effectiveness of Third-Party Consultation as a Function of the Consultant's Prestige and Style of Intervention." *Journal of Applied Behavioral Science*, 1978, *14*, 493–509.

Luke, R. A., Block, P., Davey, J. M., and Averch, V. R. "A Structural Approach to Organizational Change." *Journal of Applied Behavioral Science*, 1973, *9*, 611–35.

Miller, E. C. "GM's Quality of Work Life Efforts . . . An Interview with Howard C. Carlson." *Personnel*, 1978a, (July-August), 11–69.

Miller, E. C. "The Parallel Organization Structure at General Motors . . . An Interview with Howard C. Carlson.' *Personnel*, 1978b (September-October), 64–69.

Miller, E. C. "Measuring the Quality of Work Life in General Motors . . . An Interview with Howard C. Carlson." *Personnel*, 1978c (November-December), 21–26.

Nadler, D. A. *Feedback and Organization Development: Using Data-Based Methods*. Reading, Mass.: Addison-Wesley, 1977.

Nadler, D. A., Cammon, C., and Mirvis, P. H. "Developing a Feedback System for Work Units: A Field Experiment in Structural Change." *Journal of Applied Behavioral Science*, 1980, *16*, 41–62.

Pasmore, W. A., and King, D. C. "Understanding Organizational Change: A Comparative Study of Multifaceted Interventions." *Journal of Applied Behavioral Science*, 1978, *14*, 455-68.

Pasmore, W. A., and Sherwood, J. J. (Eds.). *Sociotechnical Systems: A Sourcebook*. La Jolla, Calif.: University Associates, 1978.

44

Porras, J. I., and Berg, P. O. "The Impact of Organization Development." *Academy of Management Review*, 1978, *3*, 249-66.

Porter, L. W., Lawler, E. E., and Hackman, J. R. *Behavior in Organizations.* New York: McGraw-Hill, 1975.

Rice, A. *Productivity and Social Organization: The Ahmedabad Experiment.* London: Tavistock, 1958.

Schein, E. H. *Process Consultation: Its Role in Organization Development.* Reading, Mass.: Addison-Wesley, 1969.

Schein, E. H., and Bennis, W. G. *Personal and Organizational Change Through Group Methods.* New York: Wiley, 1965.

Stein, B. A., and Kanter, R. M. "Building the Parallel Organization: Creating Mechanisms for Permanent Quality of Work Life." *Journal of Applied Behavioral Science*, 1980, *16*, 371-88.

Strauss, G. "Organization Development." In R. Dubin (Ed.), *Handbook of Work, Organization, and Society.* Chicago: Rand McNally, 1976. 617-85.

Tannenbaum, R., and Davis, S. A. "Values, Man, and Organizations." *Industrial Management Review*, 1969, *10* (2), 67-83.

Tolchinsky, P. D., and Woodman, R. W. "Facilitating Matrix Structures in Mental Health Using OD Techniques." Technical Report for the Florida Department of Health and Rehabilitative Services, 1981.

Trist, E. L. "On Socio-Technical Systems." In W. Bennis, K. Benne, and R. Chin (Eds.), *The Planning of Change.* (2nd ed.) New York: Holt, Rinehart and Winston, 1969.

Walton, R. E. *Interpersonal Peacemaking: Confrontations and Third-Party Consultation.* Reading, Mass.: Addison-Wesley, 1969.

White, S., and Mitchell, T. "Organization Development: A Review of Research Content and Research Design." *Academy of Management Review*, 1976, *1*, 57-73.

Woodman, R. W. "Team Development Versus T-Group Training." *Group and Organization Studies*, 1980, *5*, 135-42.

Woodman, R. W., and Sherwood, J. J. "Effects of Team Development Intervention: A Field Experiment." *Journal of Applied Behavioral Science*, 1980a, *16*, 211-27.

Woodman, R. W., and Sherwood, J. J. "The Role of Team Development in Organizational Effectiveness: A Critical Review." *Psychological Bulletin*, 1980b, *88*, 166-86.

Woodman, R. W., and Sherwood, J. J. "A Comprehensive Look at Job Design." *Personnel Journal*, 1977, *56*, 384-90, 418.

Zand, D. E. "Collateral Organization: A New Change Strategy." *Journal of Applied Behavioral Science*, 1974, *10*, 63-89.

Richard W. Woodman is an Assistant Professor in the Department of Management at Texas A&M University.

William V. Muse is Professor of Marketing and Dean, College of Business Administration, at Texas A&M University.

*The field of organization development, although
full of promise, is an emerging field still
suffering from growing pains.*

Organization Development:
Unanswered Questions

Glenn H. Varney

The field of organization development has emerged during the
last several years as an interesting and viable approach to bring-
ing about systematic change in organizations. The need for change
is made obvious to us as our environment and world economy shifts
from a traditional and stable environment to a highly reactive
and constantly changing one. Organization development has
emerged as a way of dealing with the usual confusion associated'
with change.

This chapter examines the field of organization development
(OD) in terms of this pattern of change and explores those forces that
are pushing organizations to seek the expertise of professionals in
this field. A brief historical overview is provided, and the viability of
organization development from a professional perspective is
explored. This examination requires a critical look at some of the
issues and problems surrounding organization development. The
discussion ends with some predictions for the future and some
advice regarding the use and application of OD concepts and principles to the community college.

J. Hammons (Ed.) *New Directions for Community Colleges: Organization
Development—Change Strategies,* no. 37. San Francisco: Jossey-Bass, March 1982.

Demand for Organization Development

Organization development has been defined as follows.

> Organization development is a long range effort to improve organizations, problem solving and renewal processes. Particularly through a more effective and collaborative management of organization culture with special emphasis on the culture of formal work teams, with the assistance of a change agent or catalyst and the use of theory and technology of applied behavioral science, including action research [French and Bell, 1973, p. 15].

While numerous other definitions of OD exist, the major content in this one is a clear awareness of systematic change as opposed to haphazard or casual change. In the past, the incidental character of change was a direct result of the speed with which change was taking place. Change was almost imperceptible and organizations and their members were, for the most part, unaware of it. This is not true today. The speed of change in organizations has increased at a phenomenal rate.

Stephan Fuller, a vice-president of General Motors, one of the largest corporations in the world, expresses concern over the rapidity of change today.

> Dramatic forces of change are at work in our society today. There are signs of crisis in almost every major institution. Many of these center around people; the desire of individuals for a richer quality of life in their everyday lives and on the job.

> Industrial concerns are subject to increasing pressures seeking improvement in the work force and in the environment. We hear a lot about blue collar blues, the dehumanization of workers, monotony on the assembly line, and worker alienation.

> Obviously, we in General Motors are concerned about the increasing criticism being directed toward the assembly line and other aspects of our business [1973].

Such concern from a major corporation like General Motors surely is evidence that there is a need for systematic consideration of how we deal with the human resources in organizations, rather than, as we have done in the past, force-fitting the human organization to the mechanical and technical side of business.

Friedlander explains change as a direct result of environmental factors, both social and technical, in practicing organizations. He has provided a graphic way of thinking about these changes.

A further complication we face is that the social environment is also rapidly changing. Our society now includes a work force with well-educated members who are changing their values. The work force is composed of increasingly younger people; it is estimated that approximately 50 to 55 percent is 28 years of age or younger.

Basically organizations are changing from a group of people who have traditionally been formalistic in their lifestyle (who adhere strictly to prescribed forms or rules) to a social group more concerned with its own set of values and beliefs. The term "life-style" refers to an individual's action and thoughts, which are partly unique to the person and partly shared by others. Thus, a life-style is a product of one's own culture and deliberate choices. It is often thought of as being comprised of a number of dimensions that represent various aspects of life that are common to all societies around the world. One dimension, for example, is the nature of the relationship between father and son; another is the meaning and significance of work.

Research has identified three basic classifications of life-styles. The earliest of these life-styles, referred to as formalistic, was strongest around the turn of the century. This life-style still prevails today and emphasizes rationality, control, and order in one's life. It developed along with, and was fostered by, the traditional, bureaucratic model of organization.

As technological changes became more rapid and organizations became more complex, a second life-style began to emerge. Shortly after World War II, people began to recognize the social nature of humans. Within the behavioral sciences, an entirely new field emerged called "group dynamics." Out of this social, interpersonal, group context developed industrial humanism, or human relations as we know it today. This new model of organization stresses personal growth, human dignity, work satisfaction, and democratic processes through various collaborative, interpersonal, and group relationships. It also fosters the sociocentric life-style.

48

Figure 1. The Influence of Changing Environments

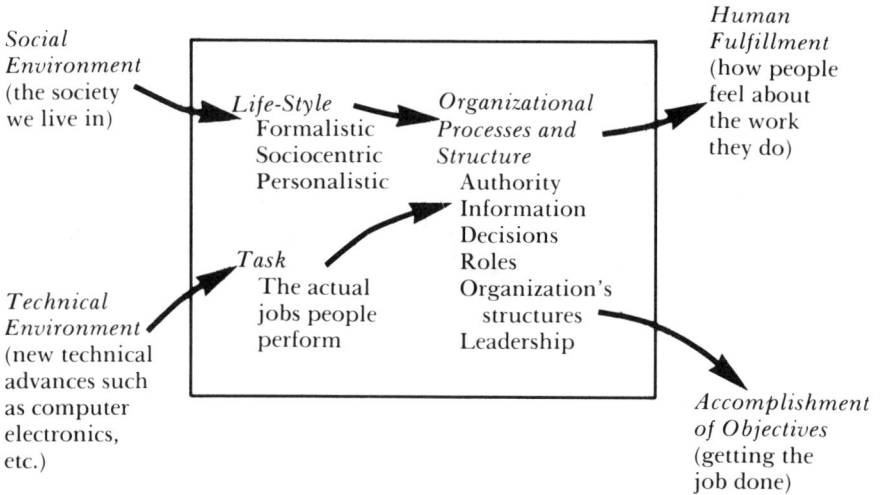

Social
Environment
(the society
we live in)

Technical
Environment
(new technical
advances such
as computer
electronics,
etc.)

Life-Style
Formalistic
Sociocentric
Personalistic

Task
The actual
jobs people
perform

*Organizational
Processes and
Structure*
Authority
Information
Decisions
Roles
Organization's
structures
Leadership

*Human
Fulfillment*
(how people
feel about
the work
they do)

*Accomplishment
of Objectives*
(getting the
job done)

(Class handout from Frank Friedlander, Case Western Reserve University. Used by permission.)

Advances in technology for the production of goods and the communication of information has led to a much more prosperous and better informed society than has ever existed. This increase in the wealth of information has led to the emergence of still another life-style, often referred to as personalistic. The personalistic life-style accepted by many younger people today is often idealistic and emphasizes personal choice and responsibility along with an integration of all the aspects of one's life.

Organizations are at least partially defined by the combined life-styles of the members of the organization. Once the organization's structure and the various processes within the structure are fairly well-stabilized, they tend to foster or develop that style of life and form of person for which they were originally designed. For instance, if an organization of 1,000 people introduced 100 new members into the organization each year, it wouldn't take more than five to ten years before the total value system of that organization would be changed. With the rapid increase of younger members in our work force, organizations are experiencing an acceleration of pressure to redefine and restructure themselves more in keeping with newer life-styles that are becoming more prevalent.

From a manager's viewpoint, a knowledge of changing life-styles is important. Administrators must be aware of the expectations of new members of an organization who have life-styles different from the present members and realize that they require different styles of managing. It is necessary to understand what kinds of conditions are required in order that individuals with different life-styles can grow and develop and maximize their work effectiveness. Managers can look at the present life-style dimensions of college students and other young people to gain some insight into the forms of organization that will be most effective at managing people in the future.

Beckhard and Harris summarize it this way: "As a result of changes in the state of the organizational world there is an increasing concern with the management of change and the need for effective strategies for changing large systems" (1977, p. 15). Although Beckhard and Harris limit their comments to changes in large systems, change takes place at all levels; not only in large systems but also in individual relationships and small groups.

Being aware of the need for systematic change as opposed to casual and incidental change is the key force that is propelling the field of organization development into the future. Roeber expresses it this way.

> Because the human environment of industry once changed slowly and in relatively predictable ways, it was possible in the past to make business decisions on the implicit assumption that this environment was constant. That is, on the assumption that the human organization was a closed system. But the environment is now changing more rapidly and in unpredictable ways. Its influence is being felt inside the boundaries of the organization and social change is becoming a factor in all business decisions [1973, p. 11].

Is Organization Development a Profession?

Like medical professionals, organization development specialists engage in the art of improving health and solving problems; however, they do so at the organizational rather than at the individual level. And, as in medicine, an incorrect diagnosis and the resulting prescription can have a devastating impact. The difference between the profession of medicine and the practice of organization development, at this state of OD's evolution, is basically the distinction between a professional and nonprofessional organization. Furthermore, when the "patient" is viewed as the entire organization of human beings (as opposed to a single individual in the case of medicine), a strong argument can be advanced for professionalizing organization development. Although organization development has not reached the professional status of, say, medicine, dentistry, veterinary medicine, or certified public accounting, it is emerging rapidly in the direction of a full-fledged profession.

Historical Perspective. Organization development mainly grew out of the academic disciplines of psychology and sociology, when applied behavioral scientists wanted to enter organizations to test their research concepts in real situations. Those initially looking for research sites were soon followed by others who approached the organization from the point of view of helping the client learn something about itself and helping it change.

As time went on, not-so-well-trained individuals were attracted to the rapidly emerging OD profession. Many of those who began to label themselves as OD consultants were from other academic fields or from personnel departments. The field had developed out of multidisciplinary philosophies, so varied backgrounds were encouraged. Readers need only look at the credentials of members in the various OD networks and OD-related organizations to see how easy it is still for almost anyone to enter this field.

The field has also resisted legal guidelines for defining what an OD professional is or does. The Certified Consultants International (CCI) maintains that statutory regulations such as licensing or certification by a state or national agency is inappropriate because of a lack of reliable and valid standards, because of a lack of knowledge about how to effectively train OD professionals, because methods for measuring a practitioner's competency do not exist, and because traditional means of disciplinary enforcement have not proven very effective (Pfeiffer, 1976, p. 373). A fear of losing the excitement of discovering different and unique change theories and strategies may stop people from developing professional standards. Many think that both professionalism and the cutting edge of discovery cannot simultaneously exist, and, faced with a choice, would opt for innovation over standards.

The client organizations must also assume some of the responsibility for this dilemma, since many are looking for quick-change solutions to very complicated problems. Their own lack of understanding of organization theory makes them vulnerable to the organizational "change artist" who has developed a flashy picture of how organizations should work and the three easy steps to achieve success.

It is one thing to recognize the need for a developmental model for OD professionals, and quite another to design it. This is particularly a problem given the range of skills and knowledge required of an effective organization development professional. Peter Vaill aptly points out that the complexities in defining what OD is (and therefore what an OD professional does) arise from the fact that OD professionals usually look at the entire organization as their province. This includes all the social and technical nooks and crannies of an organization. He states that, "the range of activities they may perform is huge; the variety of organizational circumstances in which they operate is enormous" (1971).

What is An OD Professional? We have not systematically defined what an OD professional is or does. Edgar Huse notes that "although many authors have described the personal qualities of change agents, little empirial research has been done on OD practitioner's" (Huse, 1975, p. 303). OD practitioners may describe their experiences, conjecture about what the traits of successful OD professionals are, and even define the appropriate styles to be used in varying situations. But there exists no detailed, empirically based analysis of the skills and competencies needed to succeed as an OD practitioner. The limited documentation on OD competencies consists largely of defining specific traits or talents and various rules of thumb for change agents (Shephard, 1975). In the absence of empirically based data we must rely on the judgments and opinions of experienced practitioners as our starting point.

Huse, for example, identifies the following eight personal styles and philosophies as important characteristics for OD professionals: (1) ability to assess themselves accurately, (2) objectivity, (3) imagination, (4) flexibility, (5) honesty, (6) consistency, (7) trust, and (8) stable and secure self-image. Cotton, and others identify neutrality, open-mindedness, and flexibility in processing information as the personal qualities necessary to practice OD successfully (Huse, 1975, pp. 306–9).

Partin identifies the following seven skill areas as essential for a change agent: (1) assessment of personal motivation and relationships to change; (2) helping the changee become aware of the need for change and for the diagnostic process; (3) diagnosis by the changer and changee, in collaboration, concerning the situation, behavior, understanding, and feeling for deciding upon the problem; (4) involving others in the decision, planning and implementation of action; (5) carrying out the plan successfully and productively; (6) evaluation and assessment of the changee's progress, methods and working, and human relations; and (7) ensuring continuity, spread, maintenance, and transfer of information (1973, p. 20).

Margulies and Wallace suggest several aspects of the OD consultant's behavior important to successful OD practice. These include (1) facilitating the diagnosis of problems, (2) assisting the clear statement and communication of problems, (3) pointing out those things not seen or said by the client, (4) facilitating the formulation of change plans, (5) acting as an integrator, and (6) providing internal continuity (1973, p. 141).

Criteria for Professional Status. Several criteria must be met before a field such as organization development truly can be called a profession. These include:

1. A well-developed field of specialized knowledge supported by an extensive educational system, including an accrediting process. Educational facilities should be highly standardized in the way in which they educate professionals in the field.

2. A common body of knowledge supported by extensive literature and journal documentations.

3. A licensing procedure, usually by examination, with a renewal requirement after some specified period of time. This licensing or certification procedure should be designed to maintain a level of competency for all those attesting to be professionals in the field.

4. The establishment of professional standards and ethical guidelines by which all professionals would be guided. Variation from these standards should subject the individual to censorship or possible removal of license or certification.

5. The creation of professional association that should serve as an educational, ethical, and congregating body for professionals in the field.

Issues and Problems in Organization Development

The first problem is a general lack of theory upon which the technology and practices of OD practitioners are based. For the most part, the theories that are in use come from other fields such as social psychology or sociology. Until a theoretical base is thoroughly developed it is unlikely that the field of organization development will take its place among the recognized social sciences.

Second, there are no competency measures for the educational processes which the individuals go through. Furthermore, there is relatively little consistency and agreement among the educators in the field of organization development as to precisely what an OD person should be learning. There is some common agreement around such issues as interpersonal skills and in general organizational diagnostic skills. However, the precise definitions of what constitutes a competent OD practitioner is still very much up in the air.

Third, the whole issue of whether the field of organization development is to be viewed as an analytical and rigorous researched-based process as opposed to a soft and interpersonally based process is still undecided. Much of the origin of organization development grew out of the early work of the National Training Laboratory in sensitivity training. As a direct result, two camps have formed among OD practitioners: those that are inclined towards the organizational diagnostics and those inclined towards the interpersonal side. Probably the net effect of this debate will be some sort of compromise between the two. However, the inclination on the part of organizations leans towards the more analytical practitioners.

Fourth, the whole question of evaluation of OD intervention and the effectiveness of such efforts is still an unanswered question. There have been many debates and articles written on this subject, but, as of this time, the question is unresolved. Not unlike the other recognized social science fields, organization development technology is by its very nature hard to evaluate, mainly because of the subjective character of the process and the lack of objective measures.

Community Colleges and OD

From both its acceptance and its rapid growth, it would seem that OD is here to stay. From the community college administrator's viewpoint the question is "Can OD help my college bring about an orderly change that will lead to a more effective organization and a better organizational process in the future?" Although there are many issues and concerns relative to the organization development field, OD offers as near a professional approach as can be found to systematic change. The growth of organization development over the past fifteen years shows the potential vitality of the field. The number of people who have declared themselves as OD practitioners has grown. For example, in the American Society for Teaching and Development Organization Development Division (ASTD-OD), membership has risen from 500 ten years ago to 3800 today. The same growth has taken place in the OD Network as well as other OD organizations around the world. Finally, a number of agencies, such as the Department of Labor, see the field of managing change as one of the most important vocational opportunities for young people. This is based on the expectation that this nation and its organizations will continue to go through rapid change in the next decade and will need competent help.

References

Beckhard, R. and Harris, R. T. *Organizational Transitions: Managing Complex Changes.* Reading, Mass.: Addison-Wesley, 1977.

Cotton, C. C., Brown, P.J., and Golernbrowski, R. T. "Marginality and the OD Practitioner." *The Journal of Applied Behavioral Science,* 1977, *13* (4).

French, W., and Bell, C. H., Jr. *Organization Development.* Englewood Cliffs, N.J.: Prentice-Hall, 1973.

Friedlander, F. "The Influence of Changing Environments," an 8½" x 11" model used informally in class. Case Western Reserve University.

Fuller, S., Vice President, General Motors, Corporation. Private Conversation, February 8, 1973.

Huse, E. F. *Organization Development and Change.* St. Paul, Minn.: West, 1975.

Margulies, N., and Wallace, J. *Organization Change: Techniques and Application.* Glenview, Ill.: Scott Foresman, 1973.

Partin, J. J. *Current Perspectives in Organization Development.* Reading, Mass.: Addison-Wesley, 1973.

Pfeiffer, J. W. "Perspectives." *Group and Organizational Studies,* 1976, *1* (4).

Roeber, R.J.C. *The Organization in a Changing Environment.* Reading, Mass.: Addison-Wesley, 1973.

Vaill, P. B. "Practice of Organization Development." Position Paper. Madison, Wisc.: *Organization Development Section of the American Society for Training and Development,* 1971.

Glenn H. Varney is professor of management at Bowling Green State University and President of Management Advisory Associates, Inc., a consulting firm specializing in organization development.

*The west coast director of one of the largest
national efforts toward an organization
development approach to planned change in
higher education describes the project and offers
some suggestions for other institutions.*

The Higher Education
Management Institute:
Organization Development
Through Increased
Management Effectiveness

David L. Kest

The Higher Education Management Institute (HEMI) was created
in 1976 for the purpose of designing a comprehensive management
development and training program for colleges and universities.
HEMI's primary goal was to increase the effectiveness of colleges by
increasing individual manager's skills and the understanding of
management responsiblities and functions within the institution.
The Exxon Education Foundation provided three-year funding to
the Higher Education Management Institute to support the development and testing of this comprehensive and systematic higher
education management development and training program.

Twenty-four institutions eventually were selected from more
than four hundred applicants. The number of applications received
was unanticipated; although the program was announced through
national publications, it was expected that no more than one

J. Hammons (Ed.) *New Directions for Community Colleges: Organization
Development—Change Strategies*, no. 37. San Francisco: Jossey-Bass, March 1982.

hundred institutions would apply. The pilot institutions were carefully selected to represent the diverse profile of American postsecondary education: public and private, urban and rural, large (over 10,000 student FTE) and small (under 2,000 student FTE), and two-year and four-year schools. Original planning recommended that the pilot group equally represent community colleges, four-year public universities, and private liberal arts colleges. When the final selection was completed, community colleges represented 45 percent of the pilot group.

An additional selection criterion particularly germane to this discussion was the requirement that all participating colleges and universities had to have participated in some kind of formal management/organization development activity. This was done in the belief that HEMI program success would be measurably enhanced by working with institutions previously oriented to training and development issues. Those institutions participating in the three-year pilot period contributed immeasurably to the design and effective utilization of various needs assessment instruments, training materials, and consultant services.

A major goal of the Exxon Education Foundation in funding HEMI was to ensure that the Institute would become a major force in the management development and training activities of American colleges and universities. To facilitate this role and to ensure its close association with colleges and universities and its continued development as a professional service, HEMI joined the American Council on Education as a program within the Center for Leadership Development and Academic Administration. Currently serving over 200 colleges and universities, the HEMI data base contains the results of surveys completed by over 80,000 respondents.

Organization Effectiveness

In its work with postsecondary institutions, HEMI has discovered what several researchers have described in their work on organization/management effectiveness: there is simply no single criterion or set of criteria by which to measure effectiveness. This finding was similar to that of Steers (1975) and to the conclusions of Campbell (1977). Therefore, to establish both a philosophic and programmatic foundation from which to develop its materials and services, HEMI turned to the most frequently occurring effectiveness measures of private organizations and public institutions: the overall performance of people and units, measured by personal rating;

the productivity of a unit or the institution at large, measured in actual produced data; the satisfaction of employees measured through self-reporting questionnaires; the profit of a unit or the institution as measured by accounting information; and the withdrawal of personnel, based on the rate of turnover or degree of absenteeism (Van Wijk, 1981a, p. 39).

It soon became clear that institutions in which these measures received positive ratings presented a certain organizational profile. The components of that profile are identified as the characteristics of effective management. They have become the core around which all HEMI materials and services are developed. The following section describes and provides examples of the eight characteristics of effective management.

Characteristics of Effective Management

Open Communication. This critical management skill involves listening and talking to people in such a manner as to share accurate and complete information in a supportive and friendly environment. Critical to success in this arena is ensuring that information is shared directly and in a timely fashion.

Teamwork. Time and attention must be given to creating a sense of common purpose around which colleagues choose to rally. For a sense of team identity to exist, it is essential that members of a work group share in the discussion of plans and problems and that individual contributions and participation are encouraged.

Participation in Decision Making. Work groups and institutions possessing this characteristic have clarified the roles played by various individuals and groups in the decision-making process. Actively and systematically encouraging openness, suggestions, and ideas from others is critical to success.

Encouragement of Initiative. Managers and their institutions allow considerable freedom in determining how tasks are to be accomplished. Initiative appears to operate at a high level when individual goals are congruent with the goals of the work group and the institution (Collins, 1970).

Mutual Support. Effective managers recognize and acknowledge the good performance of others. A manager's ability to minimize frustrations surrounding job content, scheduling, or resource availability greatly assists in building mutual support. An increased sense of mutual support exists when all members of the institution act quickly and effectively as problems arise.

High Standards. The standards and goals by which the institution will be measured are most effective when developed by the largest possible number of individuals. Effective institutions also work at upgrading these standards by reviewing results with members of work groups and by emphasizing the relationship between standards and performance evaluation.

Use of Objectives. The effective manager works with others to establish measurable and realistic targets and deadlines and to develop a monitoring system that accompanies the use of objectives.

Performance Evaluation. Effective managers provide timely and meaningful reactions to work performance. These managers view themselves as trainers, assisting colleagues in accomplishing a specific task and providing them with insights and recommendations for performance and/or skill development. Finally, performance needs to be evaluated based on the results achieved.

Although no single organization, and quite probably no single manager, embodies all eight effectiveness characteristics, it is the goal of the HEMI program (and a generic goal, perhaps, of any comprehensive management/organization development program) to assist educational professionals in building tangible skills within these areas. Although specifically addressing the issue of motivation, Van Wijk's observation applies equally to the concern that managers and organizations develop a wide repertoire of skills to ensure continuing effectiveness: "The important conclusion to be drawn . . . is that managers must be flexible enough to adjust their diagnostic skills to the situation; no single set of assumptions is comprehensive enough to encompass the wide range of individual behavior" (Van Wijk, 1981a, p. 28).

The following section describes how the HEMI program design reinforces, through needs assessment, data feedback, action planning, implementation and evaluation, the issues and skills reflected in the characteristics of effective management.

HEMI Program Design

The HEMI program is designed to increase organizational performance and effectiveness by increasing and developing individual management skills. An integral part of this effort has been to develop a system that allows an institution to integrate into organization development the activities of staff, faculty, and management development.

It became clear, both from shared experiences within the program design team and from a review of numerous management/ organization development programs, that to be effective HEMI had to be comprehensive and yet flexible in meeting the needs of colleges with widely varying profiles. Thus, the HEMI program is:

- *Concerned* with managers' primary responsibilities; emphasizing setting goals, obtaining and allocating resources, working effectively with people, and achieving results.
- *Specific* to higher education management. The approaches and materials used in the program have been created to meet the unique needs of higher education institutions, with enough flexibility to be adapted to different types of colleges and universities in a variety of situations and settings.
- *Organization-wide,* involving substantially all the managers in the institution, or major segments of it, in management improvement activities. All levels of managerial responsibility may be included, as well as all areas of the institution: academic, business, community, and student affairs.
- *Focused* on the unique needs of each institution, as these are identified by the institution, using survey-guided needs assessment instruments.
- *Evaluated* by each participating institution, and the institute, to ensure that results are being achieved.
- *Institution-based,* to be delivered almost entirely on-site by individuals from the institution, once they are trained to do so.
- *Integrated* into job activities to the greatest extent possible, allowing each manager to use immediately what is learned.
- *Ongoing,* intended to be used by an institution to effect real improvement in the institution's functioning.
- *Cost and time conscious,* taking into account the efficient use of managers' scarce time and the institution's budget for development and training.

The HEMI program design is based upon the involvement of work groups in campus problem solving, training, and development activities. Work groups are made up of individuals, usually from the same organizational unit, who are concerned with shared responsibilities and tasks. Work groups often meet regularly, thus developing a sense of team responsibility as they identify group objectives, relate them to the institution's goals, and support each other in accomplishing both individual and work group tasks. The role of the work group in the HEMI program design is described in the following section.

Program Phases

The program phases were designed to reinforce the notion that development and training activities ought to grow out of the needs identified by individual campus work groups. There are five phases in the HEMI program. Although most colleges will move through the phases in sequential order, the program structure allows for variation in the format described here.

Program Orientation. The first phase of HEMI involves the thorough orientation of all participants to the program goals, objectives, and mechanisms. This orientation begins with a program overview presented by HEMI to the president and senior management team of an institution. In turn, the information is shared by this group with the appropriate governing/decision-making units on campus. Once a decision has been reached to participate in the HEMI program, an institutional task force is appointed by the president. The task force represents the various functions and levels within the college management structure, often including staff and faculty representatives. The task force is trained in the use of all HEMI resources by a member of the Institute staff. Increasing widespread institutional awareness of the program and preparing individuals and work groups to complete a needs assessment instrument are initial responsibilities of the task force.

Needs Assessment Phase. Based upon the work group relationships illustrated in Figure 1, the needs assessment survey instruments collect individual perceptions of the operational functions performed within the college. The survey instruments are a direct outgrowth of the work conducted by Rensis Likert (1976). The survey results provide the data from which work group and institutional action planning can develop. Administered to the entire college community by the institutional task force, the needs assessment process provides a comprehensive review of the perceptions held by faculty, staff, students, managers, and members of the governing board. As perceptions are the realities with which individuals and institutions operate, the needs assessment process provides substantive information to be used in subsequent planning and development activities.

Figure 1. Work Groups

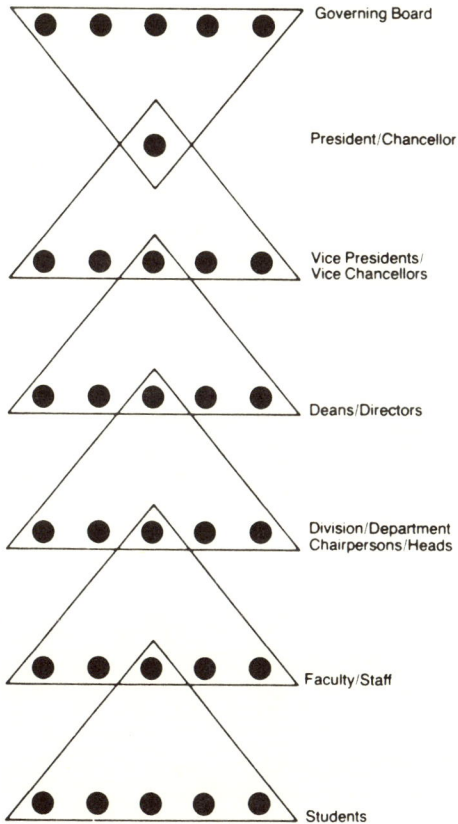

Governing Board

President/Chancellor

Vice Presidents/
Vice Chancellors

Deans/Directors

Division/Department
Chairpersons/Heads

Faculty/Staff

Students

Typical work groups for colleges and universities

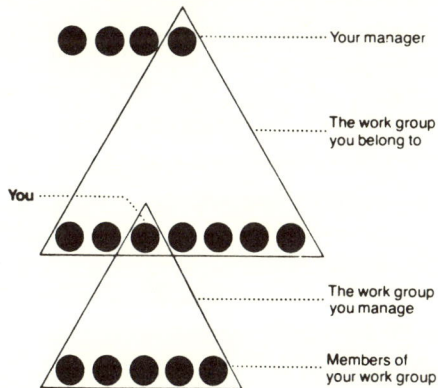

Your manager

The work group
you belong to

You

The work group
you manage

Members of
your work group

Individual–work group relationships

(Developed by the Higher Education Management Institute, Coconut Grove, Florida.)

Encouraged to candidly share their insights and attitudes, respondents are assured, through the HEMI process, of confidentiality and anonymity. Work group data belong to the individual work group, unless the group chooses to share them. Institution-wide data are reported only in summary form. The national HEMI data bank assembled from over 200 colleges and universities now constitutes a significant new information source on management/organization conditions in higher education.

Action Planning and Implementation Phase. Action planning occurs as a direct outgrowth of the needs assessment process. Individuals within work groups review data reported in the various survey categories. In addition, a work group may review the institution-wide summary data or the national data reports. Members of work groups are encouraged to review data independently and then meet with the group to determine shared concerns and recommendations for action. In addition to serving as a forum for discussing work group strengths and weaknesses and planning training and development activities, the action planning sessions encourage, often for the first time with many groups, team building and mutual support.

As part of the action planning process, each work group reviews both the various data and the HEMI program structure. The program structure establishes connections between the issues and concerns revealed in the needs assessment process and the training and development resources available through the program. For example, groups concerned with the issues of leadership and motivation may recommend that the whole group use the HEMI training modules that deal with those concerns. A group that is interested in increasing time management skills would use the HEMI Time Management Module. Work groups that see a need to better understand (or redefine) the planning process would use one of the several training modules that focus on that operational function.

Work group action plan recommendations will vary based upon the needs perceived by individual groups. Recommendations for activities will generally take one of the following forms.

Training Activities. A library of training modules has been developed to address the skill/training needs growing out of the assessment process. Intended to serve as agendas for problem solving, the HEMI training modules increase management skills while solving operational problems of the work group. Examples of training modules include "Defining Goals and Objectives," "Conducting Better Meetings," "Communication Feedback," and "Developing a Marketing Plan." All HEMI training modules are connected to the needs assessment data through the program structure.

In addition to the training modules, a series of guides have been developed to assist individual units within the institution in preparing for self-study/accreditation activities. Intended to reinforce the basic tenets of the HEMI development and training program, the guides establish connections between functions of the college, modular training activities, and the characteristics of effective management.

Developmental Activities. Recommendations in this category generally fall outside the scope of specific HEMI modular training materials. Several examples should illustrate the substance and scope of developmental activities. A work group may recommend that the role, scope, and objectives of various college task groups be redefined in order that their communication and reporting responsibilities be clarified. It is observed by the group that too frequently such task groups at the college do not communicate laterally, thus producing a duplication of effort. Another work group may suggest that standards and practices be established for staff group meetings. Such standards would include a statement of the outcomes planned, the process for distributing minutes, and the procedures to be used to insure that recommendations are implemented. Another work group may recommend that a college-wide program be initiated for crosstraining and temporary job exchange.

The action plans of individual work groups are synthesized into an institution-wide action plan for development and training activities. As a comprehensive, working document, the institution-wide action plan details strengths and concerns with accompanying recommendations for action by committees, staff, faculty, and managers.

Evaluation Phase. Evaluation of the HEMI process and its impact on an institution occurs in several ways and at various times. When initially formed, the task force, in concert with the president, develops both formative and summary evaluation criteria. The criteria are directly related to both the HEMI program objectives and the program objectives developed by and for the institution. Should the institution have as a major objective the development or refinement of a comprehensive planning system, evaluation measures are developed to chronicle the process by which the planning system will be devised, the composition of groups which will participate in the process, the target deadline through which the process will move, and the quality control factors to be used in assuring that the final planning system will serve individuals, work groups, units, and institutional goals.

Various techniques may be used for program evaluation: personal interviews, action planning documents developed by work groups and submitted to the task force, training logs detailing the specific activities and the participating groups, minutes from the ongoing meetings of the task force, and reassessment of the institution by large or specifically identified work groups.

Continuing evaluation of the HEMI process and materials occurs in several ways. A close working relationship between institutions and the HEMI staff is maintained; the training modules and guides are evaluated whenever used on a campus; the national HEMI data bank is regularly reviewed, generating new materials and publications of interest at the national level; and, the annual HEMI conference provides an opportunity for member institutions and HEMI staff to explore program successes and identify the need for new or revised materials.

Program Accomplishments

In its six-year history, the Higher Education Management Institute has worked with over 200 colleges and universities throughout the United States, Canada, and the Asian-Pacific Basin. The impact of the program, however, cannot be measured in demographics alone. Results on campuses and the impact on the larger higher-education enterprise more effectively measure the success of the HEMI program. Listed below are benefits stated by institutions utilizing the program—benefits derived from the needs assessment process, from the dialogue on each campus that develops out of systematic and comprehensive institutional assessment, from a review of the national data, and from participation in the HEMI annual conference.

- An improved understanding and acceptance of management as a process that makes it possible to use institutional resources to better advantage.
- A thorough analysis and evaluation of current operations, stimulating the institution to take a hard look at its activities and to plan changes.
- Revitalization of "meet and confer" procedures.

- Renewal of teamwork among senior executives, helping managers to think and plan as a team.
- Direction and substance for faculty and staff development programs. A variety of activities have been integrated and strengthened, and development resources have been pooled and are being used more effectively.
- Integration of human resource information as a part of the management information system. Human resources information has earned a place along with financial, operating, and student data.
- Improvement of meetings and time savings for everyone at one institution as a result of a committee study and reorganization.
- Fuller recognition of the dimensions of a nagging problem in an institution's library as a result of survey-feedback-action planning.
- A new look at the student retention problem, so that new procedures were adopted to refine retention data and new methods were established to deal with recruiting and retention as components in an integrated system.

The impact of the HEMI program on higher education is evidenced by several occurrences. Once the pilot phase of the Program was completed, the number of institutions utilizing HEMI services and materials grew dramatically (see Figure 2). With a data bank comprised of responses from over 80,000 individuals working in higher-education enterprises, HEMI has created a significant data base. The analysis of this data collection, as well as on-campus experience, has produced numerous journal articles and monographs, several doctoral dissertations, and a series of technical reports in which the raw data are analyzed.

Conclusion

As one of the first comprehensive attempts to increase management and institutional effectiveness in higher education through systematic training and development, HEMI has helped to more clearly reveal the following:

1. Institutions with similar demographic profiles often require significantly different approaches to addressing management development and training needs.
2. Program design of training and development activities must be organic to the institution, relating directly to institutional goals and objectives.

66

Figure 2. Use of HEMI Services

Number of Institutions

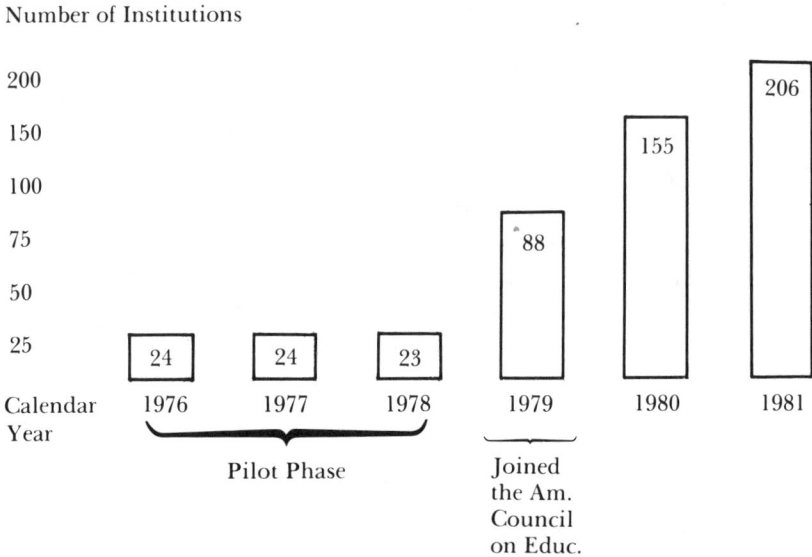

(Developed by the Higher Education, Management Institute, Coconut Grove, Florida.)

3. The process of decision making is often misunderstood and not addressed as an institutional issue.
4. The role and responsibility of the governing board are often unclear in statement as well as practice.
5. Management development and training are as critical to the effectiveness of the institution as staff and faculty development.
6. The process of institutional self-assessment is rarely connected with recommendations for development and training.
7. Management is rarely perceived as a generic function applicable to all units and levels within the institution.
8. The management profile or style of the institution is too often inconsistent with the stated mission and goals of the college.
9. Training and development activities are valued at a personal level but too often are not reinforced or encouraged at the institutional level.

10. Institutional renewal, as a phenomenon and as a prerequisite for continued effectiveness and success, is too often not approached in a programmatic manner.

Although staff, faculty, and management development activities have evolved slowly and sometimes sporadically during the past decade, organization development and the related issue of organization effectiveness may require a more intensive scrutiny and rapid implementation period. The fiscal and personnel exigencies involved in operating a college in the 1980s demand that immediate attention be directed to the issues, activities, and skills covered in an organization development program. The campus activities, the program benefits, and the data emerging from institutions participating in the HEMI Program reinforce the belief that comprehensive organization development can have a significant impact on the effectiveness and ultimate success of an institution.

References

Campbell, J. P. "On the Nature of Organization Effectiveness," in P. S. Goodman and J. M. Pennings (Eds.), *New Perspectives on Organizational Effectiveness.* San Francisco: Jossey-Bass, 1977.

Collins, R. W. "Management by Objective: Advantages, Problems and Implications for Community Colleges." Unpublished paper, University of California at Los Angeles, 1970.

Likert, R., and Gibson, J. *New Ways of Managing Conflict.* N.Y.: McGraw-Hill, 1976.

Steers, R. M. "Problems in the Measurement of Organizational Effectiveness." *Administrative Science Quarterly,* 1975, *20,* 546–58.

Van Wijk, A. *Chase Monograph 1: Assessing Managerial Functioning and Effectiveness in Higher Education. A Review of the General Literature.* Coconut Grove, Florida: Higher Education Management Institute, 1981.

David L. Kest is a director of the Higher Education Management Institute, sponsored by the American Council on Education. From 1971 to 1979 he served as a dean at De Anza College.

*A successful organization development
intervention requires a true partnership between
the players, a pervasive effort, and a climate
where change can endure.*

The National Institute:
A Partnership
for Development

George A. Baker

Organizational development is both a philosophy and a method of
influencing the behavior of organizations. It focuses on the attitudes, values, and accepted practices of people in an organization. It
recognizes that groups influence the behavior of group members
and that changes must occur in the organization's culture, particularly in the attitudes and values that organization members manifest
in the execution of their duties.

Organizational development strategies are particularly important in the community college since Henry Mintzberg places
these human resource development organizations into the family he
labels as "professional bureaucracies." Such organizations often
need external expert assistance because they are characterized by the
totally different patterns of behavior utilized by those at the top to

The author wishes to acknowledge the assistance in the development of
this chapter of John Roueche, Director of the Community College Leadership
Program and originator of NISOD; Nancy Armes, Executive Director, NISOD;
Karen Watkins, Editor, *Innovation Abstracts*, NISOD; Carol Raney, Staff
Development Specialist, NISOD; and Frances Foster, Support Staff, NISOD.

J. Hammons (Ed.) *New Directions for Community Colleges: Organization
Development—Change Strategies*, no. 37. San Francisco: Jossey-Bass, March 1982.

69

seek to control the organization and those at the bottom who seek to control their professional work without outside interference (Mintzberg, 1979).

The Dysfunctional College

When an organizational expert views the community college as a professional bureaucracy, it is difficult to determine why an organization such as this works at all. One cannot imagine a more potentially dysfunctional organization type, yet it is the structure with which the leadership and its helpers must deal.

During these difficult economic times, administrators are set upon by outside critics asking, "Why can't you control the process?" The natural response to that pressure is to tighten down the bureaucratic screws. Specifically, the administration attempts to use coordinating mechanisms such as direct supervision, evaluation systems, standardization of policies and procedures, and curriculum control measures such as competency-based instruction in order to control the process.

However, research clearly supports the notion that complex work such as that delivered by the professional cannot be effectively performed unless the intrinsic motivation is present for the person who delivers the service (Montagna, 1968). If professionals feel they are not in control of their work, both conflict and job dissatisfaction occur (Sorensen and Sorensen, 1974).

Thus, leaders of colleges are in the "damned if they do and damned if they don't" dilemma. Responding to forces demanding control, they move to increase the use of plans, rules, and codes. Often this pressure results in poor conditions for learning. Through this process, the student can come face-to-face with impersonal and ineffective professional services delivered by individuals who have lost their will to be professionals.

To change the dysfunctional college to a functional one does not proceed from a revolutionary approach; it proceeds from an evolutionary one. Change must seep in by the slow process of changing the professional who delivers the service, and change also must seep into the bureaucracy of the college. Knowing what is possible and how to proceed is the responsibility of enlightened leadership. Part of that wisdom involves seeking help from an outside agency.

Rationale for Intervention

Community colleges today are faced with much more than unstable external support systems and poor internal coordinating mechanisms. The time when customers filled classrooms to learn from dedicated professionals is behind us. Oversize budgets probably never will occur again, at least in our time. The time when stable salaries and flat operating costs existed has given way to double-digit inflation and expensive salary indexing. Meanwhile, our clients have changed from young people seeking the first two years of college to a diverse group of adult learners who want immediate payoffs for their tuition investments. As our environment and clients have changed, we have responded by increasing the size and complexity of our colleges. Cross has argued that the new adult students bring an even greater diversity to community colleges already staggering under the diversity inherent in open admissions (1980). She describes the community college dilemma as one of double add-on models. Her example of open admissions, followed by the need for developmental studies and new and expanded student services, demonstrates amply why the increased size and complexity of the community college structure exist. In a companion piece, Terry Thompson and I argued that not only must the professional be helped to deal with diversity, but the college must also deal effectively with the size and complexity issue through improved organizational and quality control processes (1981).

As colleges attempt simultaneously to cope with organizational complexity and deal with client diversity, they find themselves requiring help from the outside. The outside help must come in the form of planned change. Some argue that community colleges are ripe for organization development.

Organization Development

Organization development efforts target the beliefs and attitudes of organizational actors (Blake and Mouton, 1967). In effect, the theory of organization development seeks to reverse the typical sequence of "systems change people" to "people change systems" (Hampton and others, 1978).

To the organization development practitioner it is most important to affect positively personal values and couple these changes in personal values to changes in the ways people treat one another in the organization. Current literature supports the idea that in community colleges the general perception is that the faculty does not treat students properly, the administration does not treat faculty members properly, and in some cases, boards and publics do not treat the administration properly.

Hampton and others (1978), in summarizing the literature in organization development, present the following general model for organization development.

1. Plan the change processes with the leadership of the organization involved.
2. Change the attitudes and habits of individuals (ways people treat one another.
3. Change the group climate (the collective attitudes and habits of individuals).
4. Work out new structures (relationships between parts of the organization, tasks, and responsibilities).
5. Solve day-to-day problems involving new demands for services or new innovations.

In addition to the generalized model of organization development, there are several approaches in establishing a relationship between the helping and target institution. All of these approaches involve gathering data about the operations in the organization and the state of interpersonal attitudes and values, feedback and analysis, and team planning of new solutions and operations. The purpose of this chapter is to demonstrate how a group of change agents attempted to influence behavior in community colleges.

Prior to discussion on how the National Institute for Staff and Organizational Development (NISOD) moved to influence and improve dysfunctional aspects of prevailing attitudes, mores, and beliefs of the actors in community colleges, it is necessary to determine how all of the players formed a partnership for organization development.

A Partnership

A consortium of community colleges and NISOD became partners in development through an award of more than $1 million from the W. K. Kellogg Foundation to the University of Texas in December 1977. The foundation and the university became partners in attempting to influence the direction and quality of the community college movement in North America.

In its award letter, the W. K. Kellogg Foundation made its expectations clear. Through the award, the foundation sought to provide community colleges with inservice training of faculty and staff designed specifically around the educational needs of older, nontraditional students who must be reached through community-based programming in order to effect a significant increase in student success. In order to accomplish this mission, the W. K. Kellogg Foundation set goals designed to:

- establish a major network through the selection of pilot institutions;
- develop strategies to implement institutional change;
- develop quality products for inservice training and information;
- train community college staff to increase student success; and
- assess program impact.

Out of this genesis, the University of Texas developed an organizational structure built around the Community College Leadership Program, two external support arms, and the internal organization whose task it would be to coordinate the efforts. A description of each of the parts of the structure follows.

The Internal Partners. For approximately twenty years, the Community College Leadership Program (CCLP) at the University of Texas has provided an opportunity for prospective community college administrators to earn specialized doctorates preparing them for leadership roles in community colleges. Two key aspects of this program have resulted in the CCLP becoming the central hub of an organizational development effort. First, during its existence, the CCLP has produced more than 200 graduates. A recent analysis indicated that twenty-six of these graduates currently occupy chief executive officer positions of single campuses or multiple-campus operations. In addition, more than fifty CCLP graduates provide leadership to community colleges or community college districts while functioning at executive-level positions. It is through this network of community college leaders and more than forty others who function in teaching positions in major universities, community colleges, or in state-level public service positions that the CCLP is able to influence a central core of the community college movement. Second, the internships that are an integral part of the CCLP have allowed for direct feedback "from the trenches" as to current community college problems and opportunities. This feedback has resulted in targeted research and publications relating to the ever-changing environment in which the movement attempts to accomplish its mission.

NISOD was established as the mandated W. K. Kellogg network vehicle "to disseminate the principles, methods, and procedures utilized in community-based education programs" (Kellogg Foundation, 1977). This organization was placed within the Department of Educational Administration of the University of Texas at Austin, with organizational responsibility resting with the Dean of the College of Education. The staff was assigned under a matrix concept to both product development and field training roles, and the system allowed for the administrative planning and control necessary to concurrently develop products designed to be utilized in the field and to develop the expertise necessary to deliver the products in the field in a consulting, workshop, or conference format.

Actually, staff members of varying professional orientations combined their efforts to plan, organize, and implement workshop designs to meet individual college and regionally planned training needs. For example, staff members with task force assignments in competency-based education, microteaching strategies, leadership skills training, and module development combined their talents to design and eventually deliver a workshop on microteaching techniques for community college instructors. Concurrent product development efforts resulted in several new and innovative products designed to promote changes in the field through distributed publications. It was in moving to achieve NISOD's mission to network with its consortium through the introduction of information services that two external organizations were introduced to the partnership.

The External Partners. In October of 1978, the Fund for the Improvement of Postsecondary Education awarded a three-year grant to the Program in Community College Education at the University of Texas to develop a series of fifteen self-paced modules for community college instructors. The modules were to be developed and distributed from the University to the Kellogg Consortium. The other half of the external partnership team was formed when NISOD entered into an agreement with Media Systems Corporation, a subsidiary of Harcourt Brace Jovanovich, Inc., to publish the modules in a series entitled *The Creative Teaching Series.* It was this mechanism that would further augment NISOD's efforts in designing, producing, publishing, and marketing instructional modules to its consortium.

Later the Media Systems contract was expanded to include the publication of a minimum of thirty training modules during the three years. A unique feature of this arrangement was that not only did the strategy allow for publication of NISOD staff materials but also for those developed by faculty and administrators in the field. This strategy provided an excellent opportunity for working educators to share with others the materials and methods that they found to be successful for them. The modules themselves were developed into self-contained instructional packets including information designed to change the behavior of the reader.

The Kellogg Consortium. The keystone to the entire organization development effort was the Kellogg Consortium. It began in May 1978, as a pilot network of fifty-three community colleges, an expansion of the thirty-two directed in the W. K. Kellogg grant letter.

By September of the same year, the fifty-three colleges, divided into twelve regions, worked closely with a staff at the University of Texas that eventually numbered sixteen. From the outset, the notion of a developmental partnership was stressed. To anchor this partnership, each college would demonstrate its commitment by contributing its own staff time and money to the arrangement. Then there would be a careful negotiation process. NISOD wanted to engender the notion that membership in a developmental effort meant commitment to the goals outlined in the W. K. Kellogg grant letter. It was also important to communicate a sense of urgency to the consortium members. At each opportunity, NISOD related its purpose to its members: the idea of a partnership for sharing was the central theme.

NISOD desired to create more positive learning outcomes by combining knowledge and expertise with solid ideas through its consortium. It sought to build something new and more powerful. Through its intervention, NISOD sought to work with full-time and part-time faculty, counselors, administrators, staff, and other college personnel who influenced directly or indirectly student success in all college programs. In order to accomplish this mission, NISOD sought to organize, plan, and develop strategies around the major goals assigned in the W. K. Kellogg grant letter.

Establishing a Major Network

The NISOD focus began with individuals but sought to foster more collaboration between colleges. However, attempting to establish a network of institutions is a distinct, but important, first step in affecting the behavior of those within the college who determine student success.

The challenge for NISOD in establishing a major network was outlined by Bergquist and Lindquist when they reported that the linking agent must get to know the audience, then connect resources to the audience members at the right time and in the right way (1978).

One of the ways to excite and entice the right consortium membership is to set criteria that limit membership. The early NISOD leadership, with external advisory assistance, established such criteria. A group of colleges known for innovation and regional leadership were contacted by the project staff. The leaders of these colleges were requested to present a proposal for membership in the consortium. Presidents were asked to verify the presence of the open-door policy, an open and creative environment, a cooperative board, a stable environment, and a commitment to the investment of resources to sustain the consortium activities. Once the presidents responded to the environmental issues, most were invited to form a consortium. None of those institutions originally selected declined NISOD's invitation to join the consortium. In order to control each institution's response to the networking and training aspects, the design of the consortium called for the internal structures or organizational aspects listed below.

1. Establish a campus development team.
2. Attend at least one conference per year.
3. Provide released time for professional development.
4. Contribute to the network through product development.
5. Provide travel funds for professional development.
6. Host conferences and training sessions.

The initial group of selected colleges were invited to attend a conference at the University of Texas to orient themselves to the purposes and activities of the consortium. One of the key purposes of the conference was to gain the commitment of the college leadership to change institutional climate in ways that would improve success opportunities for students in all college programs.

Attending the conference in Austin were presidents, board members, or representatives from the original member institutions, and seven others who were subsequently identified and who had requested to attend.

One of the major outcomes of the conference was the opportunity for the college leadership to select one of four levels of involvement with NISOD.

Option A: Committed the institution to information services that would include abstracts, newsletters, modules, and conference attendance.

Option B: Committed the institution to training assistance. Each college was offered one unique workshop on campus and three mutually agreed-upon regional workshops. Also, all Option A activities were included.

Option C: Included both Options A and B. In addition, it focused on the administrative work of the college. This option included the establishment of a campus development team. Also, a planning and needs analysis visit was made to the college for the purpose of developing an institutional staff development program.

Option D: This was the most comprehensive program offered, designed to deal with total systems renewal. It involved a joint effort between NISOD and the college in the planning, management, and evaluation of all aspects of the institution that involved student success. Under Option D the planning and needs analysis would be more diagnostically oriented and would involve more areas of the college. It was expected that the president would be involved directly with the campus development team in generating energy for change.

Analysis of the decisions made by the thirty-nine college leaders attending the initial conference indicated that all but six colleges chose the level B option. The six remaining institutions chose the level C option. Other colleges made choices by telephone. It is interesting to note, however, that during the first year more than twenty of the original colleges requested a planning and orientation visit and established Campus Development Teams. These decisions resulted in these institutions escalating their level of involvement with NISOD.

Thus, the first major goal of the Kellogg charge was met, as a major network was established and remains viable at this writing. The establishment of this network also met the first criteria of the organizational development model (Hampton and others, 1978): the planning processes were commenced with the leadership of the college. Implicit in the strategy of selecting the institutions and assisting them in deciding their level of commitment was the notion of getting the leader personally committed to the purposes for which the consortium was established. It was the belief of the NISOD planners that a higher level of institutional commitment would exist if the president saw the involvement as a conscious, deliberate activity designed to improve the success opportunity for students, and that the president, through advocacy of the idea, would encourage others who might be less willing to go along with substantial changes.

The first goal was to provide the arena in which NISOD would operate with its consortium of committed and innovative colleges. The second goal of developing strategies to implement institutional change would offer a considerable challenge.

Strategies to Implement Institutional Change

The remainder of the general organizational development model (Hampton and others, 1978) would be tested in the second Kellogg goal. Strategies to implement institutional change must deal with the attitudes and habits of individuals in the college that affect group climate. NISOD would facilitate attempts to work out new structures and solve day-to-day problems in dealing with changing services to clients. These attempts were designed to deal with the dysfunctional aspects of Mintzberg's professional bureaucracy (1979). Strategies to implement institutional change revolved around several initial efforts by the NISOD staff. These strategies included cultivating the staff developer, performing a needs analysis, forming a campus development team, designing local and regional workshops, and establishing a summer institute.

The Staff Developer. Member institutions committed themselves to two crucial components in joining the Consortium. The first commitment was that the chief executive officer would publicly endorse the ideas behind the Kellogg Consortium and would commit the institution to the planning processes necessary to deal with the aspects of the general organization model. The second commitment was that a professional on campus was to be released for at least one-third of his or her time to coordinate the activities linking NISOD, the institution, and other consortium members. The key role to be played by this contact person, who in almost all cases became the institutional staff development officer, was NISOD's contact person and its day-to-day linkage to the college.

Descriptions of these staff development/NISOD contacts varied significantly: some were professional faculty who had been given release time, some were administrators involved in instructional supervision, and in a few cases a staff developer already existed in the college structure and was assigned the additional role of NISOD coordination. In more than one case, the president acted in the additional role as staff development/NISOD coordinator.

Some of the contacts were experienced staff developers; others had no previous experience in operating staff development programs or in playing a role of contact person between the college and NISOD. However, it was this contact person who, more than any other aspect of the program, became the sine qua non of the change effort.

Needs Analysis. Once the college and its leadership were committed to change, some mechanism was needed to determine what needed changing. An important approach to solving this problem was gathering data about the state of operations at the organization being assisted. Early in the effort, needs assessment instruments were sent to each member institution. These instruments were developed from research that yielded competencies reported by staff and faculty as highly desirable. These competency goal statements also became preliminary product development goals for NISOD in its product development effort. In this preliminary data-gathering phase, individuals from all areas of the institution responded to specific competency goal statements listed under the series of workshops that NISOD had begun to develop. The purpose of this activity was to solicit the most comprehensive assessment possible by gathering perceived needs from various individuals, departments, and divisions at each college. These preliminary data on the present and desired levels of each area were employed by NISOD and institutional representatives in developing and conducting more realistic planning sessions for involvement with NISOD and in realizing a more relevant consortium design and implementation strategy.

Not only were these data collection efforts important to NISOD, they provided planning information to the institution. One of the key problems in early organization development efforts was the little evidence supporting the conclusion that individuals who had been exposed to management training had changed attitudes or values when they returned to work. The early approach to organization development proceeded from the premise that if leaders changed, subordinates would surely follow (Mann, 1957).

NISOD sought to improve on these early efforts by focusing on individuals, groups, and college-wide performance. Therefore, competency goals were stated broadly enough to relate to the behavior of individuals, groups, and in some cases, institutional problems. Every attempt was made to ensure that survey results were dealt with by task forces who represented every aspect of a problem. The needs analysis technique not only met the overall goal of the Kellogg Foundation to improve the success opportunities of students in all programs of the college, it met the major goals of the organization development model by assisting institutional members to examine their relations with one another, improving the collective attitudes and norms of individuals, and, most importantly, attacking day-to-day problems by attempting to work out new structures to better support student learning.

The Campus Development Team. Another key change that began to develop in many NISOD colleges was the ad hoc task force called the campus development team. As has been pointed out elsewhere in the chapter, despite awareness of the need for interdependence in order to effectively serve students' needs, colleges have generally focused on various parts of a problem as opposed to the larger issue. As reported by Comstock and Mink (1979), these various parts may be programmatic and bureaucratic. On the professional side of the college, one can change personnel, reorganize the curriculum, or reallocate space. On the bureaucratic side of the college, one can allocate space and resources, establish policies and procedures, and establish means of controlling the process. However, the college rarely interacts to ensure the smooth functioning of the organic whole.

The idea for the campus development team (CDT) grew out of the application of action research concepts as discussed by Sikes and others (1974). The rationale for applying the team concept related to the inability of the organization to meet the needs of both the client and the professional by looking simultaneously at their various needs. Through the commitment to the tenants of the consortium and the planning and orientation visit, NISOD assisted colleges to assemble individuals who would work with presidents, faculties and staffs, staff developers, and external agents in the development and execution of change strategies.

The CDTs were composed of individuals most involved with the notion of improving student success. The teams provided a central focus for problems that had historically been ignored by the various parts of the college. The central core of CDTs included faculty, staff, midlevel administrators, students, and others. Because of the ad hoc nature of the CDTs, there was open discussion of problems or challenges, a central core to mobilize activity to carry out agreed-upon change projects, and the informal power necessary to increase the ownership of problems through the incorporation of broader concerns. The benefits of the CDTs included personal growth of individuals, an increased awareness of self, unity, and the general condition on campus.

Those who assisted in establishing CDTs verified the findings of Gaff (1975), who reported the attributes enhanced by the CDT were open and trusting relationships; widespread participation in decision making; encouragement of administration, faculty, and staff to be self-directed and responsible for their actions; encouragement of personal growth; acceptance of institutional diversity; an opportunity to deal with conflict; and the opportunity to deal with feedback in a nonthreatening manner.

CDTs took major responsibility for the analysis of the data provided by NISOD. In most cases, the CDT became the planning task force to work with the staff developer in executing the responsibilities previously mentioned. It is easy to see why the CDTs not only became the central force for change on campus, but also were extremely active in all phases of NISOD's training and information-sharing strategies.

Local and Regional Workshops. From the beginning of the project, it was apparent that one of the most ambitious undertakings of the Kellogg charge was training the community college staff toward the goal of increased student success. In this challenge, all of the aspects of the general model for organization development would be operating. One series of workshops would be developed to assist in planning change processes, another series would deal with changing the attitudes and skills of individuals, and a third series would deal with group climate. A fourth group would address relationships between parts of the organization. It was envisioned that these sets of targeted workshops would contribute to solving day-to-day problems toward increasing the success opportunities of students. Since most of the colleges had committed to Option B, it was clear that the training assistance notion was valued by Consortium members.

At the time that NISOD staff was beginning to develop training products based on a macroanalysis of the consortium's competency-goals decisions, staff members who worked with each region of the consortium were engaging in planning with institutional presidents and staff developers regarding the planning and orientation visit. A pervasive model brought the staff development officer and the CDT (or a task force that ultimately constituted the CDT) together with the regional coordinator from NISOD.

In addition to the analysis of the needs assessment data, it was typically the role of this group to decide on the campus workshop and to collectively plan, through the regional coordinator, for the regional workshops. Since regional coordinators also played a role in the development of workshops, they were rather persuasive in assisting the institution to make choices. Two early workshop favorites involved planning for change. They were "Building a Staff Development Program" and "The Campus Development Team." Regional workshops tended to focus on the individual change notion and consisted of such workshops as "Analyzing Teaching Techniques," "Building Successful Communication in the Classroom," or "Creating a Positive Learning Environment." Other workshops were designed to affect the attitudes and values of a particular element of the college such as the student services division or a curriculum department of the college. Workshops in this series included "Improving Developmental Studies," and "Personalized Competency-Based Curriculum Development." A key set of workshops dealt with relationships between parts of the organization. Examples of these workshops were "Improving Student Retention" and "The Student Development Model." Another set of workshops sought to deal with improving individual attitudes and skills but were generalized to the degree that a wide spectrum of participants could interact; examples are "Communication Skills" and "Leadership Styles, Locus of Control, Reality Therapy and Consulting Skills." Two workshops were designed for mid- and top-level managers to improve the attitudes and skills of administrators in the strategic arena. The titles of these workshops were "The Role of the Administrator in Managing Change" and "Utilizing Human Resources Effectively." While these workshops were designed for campus and regional use, NISOD sought to develop strategies that were more global in nature; one such strategy was the annual NISOD Summer Institute.

The Summer Institute. A unique training and information-sharing opportunity offered by NISOD to its member institutions has been the annual Institute on Staff Development and Conference of Presidents. Held at the University of Texas at Austin campus, the concurrent programs of the institute and president's conference provide opportunities for chief executive officers, staff developers, and college faculty from all parts of the U.S. and Canada to come together and exchange the best and most recent information on staff development issues and practices. Nationally recognized experts and NISOD staff members address current and future trends and techniques. Perhaps of even more importance has been the opportunity for participants to establish networks for information and program concept sharing with their counterparts from the broad cross section of the institutions represented in the Kellogg Consortium.

The 1981 Institute on Staff Development and Conference of Presidents, held in May, was titled "Confronting Complexity: Developing Community Resources for the 80s" and focused on the creation and expansion of community resources to enlarge networks, strategies to mobilize colleges and communities to more powerfully serve the educational needs of adults, and exploration of issues and trends affecting higher education in the 1980s. Participants were involved in skill-building sessions on staff management programs, planning, and developmental tasks as well as hearing the thoughts of recognized experts in the community college field discuss their perceptions of forces affecting community college development in the next several years. The 1981 institute and conference were cosponsored with the Texas Association for Community Service and Continuing Education. The addition of continuing education and community resource development personnel from various Texas colleges enhanced both the program opportunities available during the Institute and the networking possibilities available to our own NISOD consortium members.

Developing Quality Products

The third major goal of the Kellogg Foundation was to develop quality products for in-service training and information sharing. NISOD's product development efforts resulted in two information service publications.

The Creative Teaching Series. An important component of NISOD's communication with Kellogg Consortium member colleges has been the development and dissemination of a series of self-paced instructional modules for community college faculty members. The Creative Teaching Series modules, funded by the Fund for the Improvement of Postsecondary Education, were to be developed from research results and from theories that had proved beneficial to the teaching/learning process. The modules were to translate theory into practice, to be as free of jargon as possible, and to provide enough theoretical background for understanding the concepts contained in each module—the "why" behind the "how." Most of the material involves practical, skill-building exercises designed to provide instructors with new tools to use with nontraditional learners. The modules were developed by members of the NISOD staff as well as experts in community college development

84

and research and expert practitioners in the field. An agreement with Media Systems Corporation in New York, a subsidiary of Harcourt Brace Jovanovich, resulted in the publication of a polished, professional product.

Although the printed materials available to Kellogg Consortium members were originally viewed as supplemental to on-site training activities and training telephone consultations, the modules and other printed services offered consortium members have grown in popularity and importance in the past several years. Inflationary costs affecting college employees' and consultants' travel expenses and the growing recognition of the need for a continuing availability of staff development information have increased the impact of these publications and the total package of printed services to our members.

To date, over 10,000 Creative Teaching Series modules have been distributed to community colleges in the U.S. and Canada. It is anticipated that the number of users will continue to grow as additional modules become available and more extensive use of the modules is encouraged on individual college campuses. Originally, these booklets were designed to be used as supplements to training activities; now however, the modules have become the basis for many ongoing staff development experiences for college instructors. The Creative Teaching Series modules constitute a continuing, tangible legacy of the relationship between the NISOD staff based in Austin and its member institutions across the U.S. and Canada.

Innovation Abstracts. The other information partner has been the highly successful *Innovation Abstracts* series. Over the life of the project, this series has continued to be a central part of NISOD's information services to consortium members. A key incentive to the NISOD staff has been the series' excellent reception and the increasing number of submissions from the field, which reinforces the sense that the *Innovation Abstracts* have now taken their place as a relatively regular and routine feature of the community college landscape.

Recently, a survey of abstracts authors was conducted to determine the extent of follow-up they have received from NISOD's readership. The surveyors were amazed to discover that although several authors reported receiving no follow-up, a large number had received anywhere from five to one hundred calls or comments. Naturally, those people who in their abstract indicated that further information was available were the ones most likely to receive requests for that information. One of the happy findings in this early stage of data analysis is that program-level innovations were highly represented among those that received the most requests for information.

NISOD recently received an additional grant from the Fund for the Improvement of Postsecondary Education to develop a special twelve-issue series of *Innovation Abstracts* called the "Federal Project Series." This series will highlight exemplary practices that have been funded at the federal level and that have particular interest for educators in community colleges.

One final indication of the response of member institutions to the abstracts is the incredibly large percentage of consortium members who renewed with NISOD in the past year in time to receive the bonus of 100 copies of each issue. This response is seen as indicating the ongoing appeal of the abstracts to the Consortium.

Training Community College Staff

The fourth goal of the Kellogg charge was to provide training to community college staff members. Much of this effort has been covered under change strategies; however, it is important to consider how this change strategy changed over the life of the project.

Education, renewal, and revitalization comprise three key elements of NISOD's major training goal for the nation's community college faculty and staff. Although it is an established fact that community college enrollees are characterized by learning deficiencies in the basic skills and by a broad range of self-defeating behavior patterns, many educators remain unprepared to deal with the demands of these students. During the project years 1977 to 1981, NISOD staff created (and continues to create) a variety of staff development training programs and consulting services to meet the nontraditional challenges facing community college personnel.

However, the staff development emphasis has been refocused. Inflation and reduced operating budgets have plagued nearly all member colleges. The cost of air transportation has nearly doubled in one brief year. These financial factors have caused a dramatic reduction in the number of staff development requests to NISOD. As a result, NISOD moved to execute training through external resources, expanding its training capabilities by using many people who had attended NISOD workshops in the past and who also desired to provide training outside their own institutions. The adjunct model has been in effect since the first year and seems to be working satisfactorily.

NISOD has provided 120 workshops during the past three years to its network members and has trained more than 5,000 participants—faculty, counselors, and administrators. Workshop evaluations indicate that acceptance continues to be high. Using a 1 to 6 rating scale, with six being the most positive score, the average is well above five in composite scores, with the highest scores coming under the categories of "relevancy of ideas and activities" and "effectiveness of workshop leaders." Even with high workshop evaluations, NISOD has sought ways to lower the cost of offering training.

Since there are not as many funds available for travel expenses and training fees associated with putting together an effective workshop experience, NISOD has suggested the (1) sharing of expenses among institutions in close proximity to each other, and (2) planning of workshop schedules so that NISOD trainers can lead several workshops during one trip and institutions can share travel costs. As NISOD began the consortium, the basic service offered was a training service. The realities of the 1980s dictate that training now be seen as a support service, important but no longer the main enterprise of the staff development undertaking.

It is also clear that some of the early workshop efforts are now being modeled by various professional staff members in the field. That which NISOD once provided is now being provided on a district and regional basis by professionals who have followed its lead. In searching for evidence of impact from the field, being modeled is the most positive compliment the organization can receive.

Assessing Program Impact

The final Kellogg goal was to assess program impact in the field. The Kellogg Project is currently evaluating long-term effects of its staff development efforts in selected consortium colleges. By identifying specific behaviors or activities advocated by Kellogg consultants in earlier staff development workshops and assessing their current use by workshop participants, the goal is to trace the "staying power" of the training.

A questionnaire has been developed for workshop participants to report their use of specific strategies to improve student learning and retention. A parallel questionnaire for administrators who did not participate in the training workshops has also been designed. The administrative questionnaire seeks to elicit four types of information: (1) the administration's perception of the frequency of use of certain activities by faculty and staff, (2) his or her perception of the length of time the faculty and staff have used the activities, (3) the type of involvement the administrator has with the activities, and (4) the kind(s) of experiences which have influenced the administrator's involvement with the activities. The questionnaires will also offer an opportunity to analyze the impact of related Kellogg materials in relationship to staff development efforts in the consortium by assessing the influence of *Innovation Abstracts* and the Creative Teaching Series on administrator support and workshop participant behavior change.

It is not enough to say that NISOD will expend major efforts in its fifth year to determine its effectiveness. Existing patterns can be examined to determine measures of success. The first pattern is the evolution of information services. Initially, the paper flow efforts sponsored by NISOD for the consortium were designed to supplement a more intensive training program, but as the fourth year of the network is completed, it is becoming more clear that the reverse has occurred. NISOD has become a clearinghouse for information about teaching and learning for adults, which it in turn provides to the consortium as its staple service. NISOD-sponsored training has remained a healthy function used often by our member schools but less frequently requested than during its first three years.

A second pattern that has established itself is the staying power of the consortium itself. It began as a pilot network of 53 institutions; currently one hundred forty institutions are members, forty-two of the charter institutions are still members, sixty-two institutions have been members for more than a year, and in the last ten months, thirty-six new institutions have joined. Today, NISOD's consortium is a healthy mix of new and old. However, the most encouraging single fact of the membership pattern is that once an institution joins, in two of three instances, it will remain for more than a single membership year. A corollary benefit of staying power is that NISOD is developing a community of educational innovators who know each other and who know NISOD staff at the University of Texas. Perhaps the most important imperative for the future is to make sure that new member institutions joining the consortium are quickly acclimated to the nature of the network.

What We Have Learned

Much has been learned from the NISOD effort about the nature of building an effective development program for educational professionals. The movement is not exactly where it was envisioned it would be, yet the staff has learned what is important and relevant for those who seek to make change from the outside.

Looking back, what seemed to occur and what is now part of the staff development model was the formation of a personal network involving presidents, contact persons, key faculty members on the campuses, and NISOD staff. At that vulnerable point, as work began, professionals of power and influence lent credibility to the training and consulting efforts. In essense, NISOD formed a personal network and built reciprocal relationships based on face-to-face encounters. Forming such a network within a network has served the organization well and, in fact, became a true foundation.

In the second year, the organization became the National Institute for Staff and Organizational Development (NISOD) and issued an open invitation to all community colleges to join the network. Within the year, the group doubled in size and then tripled during the two years following the open invitation. As a fifth year begins, there is every reason to believe such growth will continue.

NISOD's actions to adapt its services to meet the needs of this larger group are very important. The organization was adapted in sizable and pervasive ways. Analysts of change might well designate the change agents' behavior to have been high risk. In actuality, it was inevitable. Partly, NISOD adapted in its second and third years because money available for travel began to be severely limited and it was impossible to schedule as many face-to-face encounters. If staff members could not be present in person, at least their ideas could. It was difficult to anticipate that something so simple as frequent, regular paper contact would bolster NISOD's efforts, perhaps more than any other one ingredient) after a firmly established foundation based on face-to-face encounters was in place.

In these efforts, something interesting was learned about the effect of publications. If they are carefully targeted, they tend to be less threatening than frequent direct encounter and yet they keep interest alive. This is an unexpected outcome, but one the staff has given considerable thought to. The lesson is that a message delivered in writing gives space and reaction time, especially to the weary or wary professional, and yet has the potential to offer a much-needed encouraging word.

Another concern was how to foster such primary networking within member institutions. Basically, the goal was to provide several different opportunities to nourish the process. Workshops were developed that encouraged the formation of small units within the college that would work toward common staff development goals. If the workshop went well, a bonding occurred among the group and between the group and NISOD and all the tasks were simplified. Another tactic was to encourage a few of the professionals who were especially interested in staff development to travel together under a common purpose: to make a site visit at a college with an innovative program, to participate in a regional conference or workshop where kindred spirits gathered, or to attend the Staff Development Institute held in the spring at the University of Texas.

Surprisingly, even over long distances, it could be determined rather easily whether these internal networks had either formed or failed to form. For one thing, returning faces could be counted. For example, during the three years of the Summer Institute, approximately 50 percent of the professionals interested in staff development returned. In part, the internal networks had formed by an interesting ripple effect that occurred where one introduced another, who introduced another, to form groups of similarly included educators. This patterned growth, like a chain-link fence, evidences strength.

This strength is at the heart of the organization development process—the central mass of the organizational essence that must be moved. As the central mass moves, the strength increases. These increases were incremental but foundational. Leaders were involved from the beginning and strategies were oriented to changing the ways individuals treated one another. As individuals changed, groups began to change; as groups changed, the structure began to change to support group expectations. Gradually, day-to-day problems were faced with new energy and resolve.

Of course, there is no means to measure the extent to which the external forces reshaped internal forces. Often, the NISOD experience was only one of the major forces that community colleges chose to react to. Nevertheless, as the late 1970s are examined in the future, it will be evident that many community colleges began to develop unique personalities with the help of organizations dedicated to producing measured change.

References

Baker, G. A., III, and Thompson, T. R. "Coping With Complexity: A Challenge for Open-Door Colleges," *Community College Frontiers*, 1981, *9* (2) 26–32.
Bergquist, W. and Lindquist, J. "Dissemination Through Networking," in J. Lindquist (Ed.), *Increasing the Impact of Social Innovation Funded by Grant-making Organizations*. Battle Creek, Mich.: W. K. Kellogg Foundation, 1978.

90

Blake, R. R., and Mouton, J. S. "Grid Organization Development." *Personnel Administration*, January-February, 1967.

Comstock, V. N., and Mink, O. *Campus Development Teams*. Austin: The University of Texas, NISOD Working Paper, 1979.

Cross, K. P. "Dealing With Diversity," Address at the American Association of Community and Junior Colleges, San Francisco, March 1980.

Gaff, J. G., *Toward Faculty Renewal*. San Francisco: Jossey-Bass, 1975.

Hampton, David, Summer, C., and Webber, R. *Organizational Behavior and the Practice of Management*, (3rd ed.) Glenview, Ill.: Scott Foresman, 1978.

Kellogg Foundation letter of December 28, 1977, from A. E. Elser to Donald Walker, Chancellor of the University of Texas.

Mann, F. C., "Studying and Creating Change." In C. Arensberg and Associates (Eds.), *Research in Industrial Human Relations*. New York: Harper and Row, 1957.

Mintzberg, H. *The Structuring of Organizations*. Englewood Cliffs, N.J.: Prentice-Hall, 1979.

Montagna, P. D., "Professionalization and Bureaucratization in Large Professional Organizations," *American Journal of Sociology*, 1968, 74 138–45.

Sikes, W. W., Schlesinger, L. E., and Seashore, C. N. *Renewing Higher Education From Within: A Guide to Campus Change Teams*. San Francisco: Jossey-Bass, 1974.

Sorensen, J. E., and Sorensen, T. L. "The Conflict of Professionals in Bureaucratic Organizations." *Administrative Science Quarterly*, 1974, *19* 98–106.

George A. Baker, Director of the National Institute for Staff and Organizational Development, also teaches in the Community College Leadership Program at the University of Texas at Austin.

Survey feedback could be one of the most useful and effective OD interventions available to community college personnel.

Survey Feedback: An Effective OD Intervention

Gordon E. Watts

Organization development, as we have discovered, is a planned change process that has as its ultimate goal increased organizational effectiveness. The methods, techniques, and structured activities that constitute the process and in which members of the organization participate are called OD interventions (French and Bell, 1979). They are, in other words, the tools of the trade.

One of the most widely used OD interventions (Nadler, 1977) is called survey feedback, which has been described as follows:

A type of data-based intervention which flows from surveys of the members of a system on some subject and reports the results to the group" [Varney, 1977, p. 221].

A process in which data is systematically collected (normally by questionnaires) from members of an organization, analyzed in summary fashion, and fed back selectively to organization members" [Friedlander and Brown, 1974, p. 326].

A procedure in which outside consultants and members of a system collaboratively gather, analyze, and in-

J. Hammons (Ed.) *New Directions for Community Colleges: Organization Development—Change Strategies,* no. 37. San Francisco: Jossey-Bass, March 1982.

terpret data that deal with various aspects of the system's functioning, and its members' professional lives. Using such data as a base, the participants, with consultative help, begin problem-solving efforts to improve the organization processes and the working relationship among members" [Schmuck and Miles, 1971, p. 113].

These descriptions contain the essence of the three major components of survey feedback. The first two components, as illustrated by the first two descriptions, are the use of a survey or questionnaire to gather information from members of an organization and the feedback of survey results to those who completed it. The third component involves discussing the results of the survey and planning action to overcome or alleviate those factors identified as hindering group or organizational effectiveness.

The use of surveys or questionnaires in the community college is not uncommon. However, there are distinct differences between the typical approach to the use of surveys and the approach used in survey feedback. According to French and Bell (1978), the typical approach is to gather data from only a certain segment of the organization, usually the lower levels in the hierarchy. The results are then seen only by the top administrators and perhaps by some mid-level administrators with no assurance or commitment that the results will be put to any practical use. In survey feedback, on the other hand, everyone is usually included in the survey and everyone receives the results. Further, the results are discussed in work teams that involve everyone, and there is a definite commitment to developing action plans.

Organization development, as Hammons points out in an earlier chapter, refers to changes in the technology and structure of an organization, in individuals and the ways in which they interact with one another, and in the organization's interactions with its environment. The surveys and questionnaires utilized in survey feedback, therefore, focus on one or more aspects of the structure, processes, and interactions of the organization and its members. Some surveys cover one topic or aspect and others take a multifaceted approach to measurement. Common focal points of surveys are the allocation of authority and responsibility, the establishment of clear goals and communication networks, effective decision making, problem-solving techniques, methods of conflict management and resolution, general organizational climate, leadership, trust and openness, planning, team work, cooperation versus competion, and motivation.

Typical examples of items found on surveys are as follows:

Statement: Generally, this institution has well-established formal communication channels.

Scale: Don't know   Unsure, probably agree
Not applicable   Unsure, probably disagree
Agree   Disagree

(Anderson, 1981)

Statement: Are professionals involved in decisions related to their work?

Scale: Almost never   Generally consulted
Occasionally consulted   Fully involved

(Likert, 1967)

Statement: Do you feel a responsibility to help this institution meet its goals?

Scale: Completely   To a little extent
To a very great extent   To a very little extent
To a great extent   Not at all
To some extent

(Hadley and Andrews, 1978)

The Advantages of Survey Feedback

When looking at the variety of OD interventions available and the pros and cons of each, the popularity of survey feedback becomes apparent. For example, one of French and Bell's (1978) classifications of interventions indicates that survey feedback is one of only four interventions that can deal with both task (what the organization is doing) and process (how it is doing it) dimensions of groups within the organization. In addition, French and Bell classified interventions according to which of five different organization units—individuals, dyads/triads, teams and groups, intergroup relations, and the total organization—they could expect to affect. Survey feedback was the only intervention designed to improve the effectiveness of the last three units. The potential for survey feedback to have a positive, far-reaching effect on the organization is thus greater than for any of the other interventions.

Survey feedback affords some other advantages. First, since organizational members are usually involved in the choice of survey instruments or in their design, there is more personal involvement in the feedback sessions and less perceived threat from the data. Consequently, group members tend to be more committed to the planning process, more motivated to change, and more committed to implementing any changes that are planned. In addition, by establishing times for periodically readministering the survey, the organization can monitor the progress of change and assess the change process itself. Again, commitment to change is enhanced, especially if group members know beforehand that follow-up is part of the process.

On the technical side, collecting data through surveys is usually fast, easy, and economical, and large numbers of participants can be surveyed without slowing the process appreciably. Finally, results from surveys lend themselves easily to statistical use so that feedback is facilitated and comparisons can be made not only across groups but also with norm groups.

Some Shortcomings of Survey Feedback

One major disadvantage of survey feedback is the possibility that it could be used improperly. An administrator with only self-serving purposes in mind, for instance, could use information from a survey as ammunition against someone that he or she wished to dismiss. Administrators could also misuse survey data to support their own particular perceptions, issues, or contentions to the exclusion of anyone else's. Such misuse would clearly promote adversary relationships within the organization and would be detrimental to survey feedback's intended purpose of effecting positive growth and change within the organization.

Other disadvantages of using the survey feedback approach are problems associated with the survey itself. First, surveys are rather impersonal and as such are subject to misinterpretation. Further, since the questions are predetermined, they may miss the crucial issues altogether. Surveys can also elicit reactions from the participants such as anger, fear, trying to outguess the survey, and answering in socially desirable ways that tend to cloud the validity of the results. Some of these reactions may carry over into the feedback sessions so that excessive time is spent on surface issues such as criticizing the instrument and not in real problem-solving activities. On the other hand, the data could be overinterpreted so that group members make inferences and judgments that are not supported by the data.

Results from Research

The results of research conducted on survey feedback support its widespread use as an OD intervention. In one of the most notable studies, Bowers (1973) compared the impact over time of four OD interventions on a variety of variables in twenty-three organizations. He found that only survey feedback and interpersonal process consultation had a positive impact on a majority of the organizational measures being studied, and survey feedback was the only one that improved organizational climate.

Also, Friedlander and Brown (1974), who conducted a thorough review of the research literature on OD, found research that suggested that the effectiveness of survey feedback was increased when group members were involved in the design and collection of data, when managers of the groups were actively involved in the problem-solving/planning process, when an outside consultant facilitated the process, and when decisions about follow-up and action steps were specific.

How to Use Survey Feedback Effectively

To use the survey feedback methodology effectively requires more than simply administering a survey, returning the results, and planning action steps. This section, therefore, draws on the works of Bowers and Franklin (1977), Fordyce and Weil (1971), French and Bell (1978), and Nadler (1977) to provide a more in-depth view of the survey feedback process.

Setting the Stage. Like any other change effort, survey feedback should not be initiated unless there are strong indications that change is needed. Once that need is acknowledged, the president of the college (or appropriate top-level administrators) must be committed to the effort and willing to expend resources, both human and material, to complete the project. The administration must also realize that the entire process should be jointly planned and designed by representatives from all levels of the organization that are to be included in the process.

The Resource Person. Before proceeding further, a decision should be made regarding the use of a resource person or consultant. Most proponents of survey feedback suggest that a resource person be utilized throughout the entire process. The person could assist in defining the purposes of the intervention, selecting or designing a survey instrument, and analyzing the survey results. The person also would play a key role in feedback sessions which will be explained in more detail later in this section.

The roles and activities that a resource person is involved in are varied and range from facilitating group processes to planning to analyzing complex data. Selecting the right resource person, therefore, is an important decision and should be done with care. Briefly, the resource person should be skilled in OD and human relations. He or she should also be flexible enough to adapt to the demands and characteristics of the situation and be cognizant of the need to keep the process moving at a steady pace. The interested reader can refer to Hammons and Hunter (1977) or Bell and Nadler (1979) for further information on the role and selection of consultants and resource persons.

Determining the Purpose. The next part of the process is to determine a clear purpose for the survey. Data should not be gathered just for the sake of gathering data nor to accommodate the self-serving purposes of some misguided administrator. Rather, the purpose should be to improve the effectiveness of those areas where survey feedback is best suited as an intervention; i.e., teams and groups, intergroup relations, and/or the total organization. The factors and conditions that created the impetus for change would then give rise to a more specific definition of the purpose.

Selecting a survey instrument. Once the purposes are set and the topics or areas of concern selected on which data are to be gathered (such as leadership, problem solving, communications, planning, climate, etc.), the appropriate survey instrument can be selected. The alternatives available at this point are to select an existing survey and use it without modification, modify an existing survey, or generate a new survey instrument.

If an existing survey is selected, it is important to be certain that the survey measures what you want measured. A review of the survey will establish its validity and a review of any available manuals or other supporting documents will help determine if the type of results expected from the survey will be useful. Then it is necessary to determine, if possible, the stability of the survey. Pfeiffer, and others (1976) suggest that any instrument should have a reliability coefficient of .85 or higher to provide assurance that the results will be accurate.

Selecting an existing instrument and making modifications (such as changing the language to fit a community college setting) has the advantage of creating a more appropriate survey while retaining the same validity and reliability as the original instrument.

The main advantage of designing your own instrument is, of course, that it can be designed to meet specific needs and circumstances. It can be comprehensive or specific, long or short, and follow whatever format is best for the situation. On the other hand, it takes more time and effort to design an instrument, and it should be pilot-tested for reliability. Recently, however, a self-designed survey was successfully developed at Los Angeles Southwest College for their use in OD (Hadley and Andrews, 1978). In their paper, the authors describe the process they used to design the instrument and determine its reliability. They indicate, too, that for the most part, the survey can be used in other community colleges. For other outlines and descriptions of how to design a survey instrument, refer to Varney (1977) or Pfeiffer and others (1976).

Other Determinants. Another aspect of selecting an instrument is cost. The out-of-pocket cost of the survey should be taken into account as well as the cost for scoring the survey. A closely related aspect is time. The length of time needed to complete and score the survey is a determining factor. Also, as noted above, time is a factor if the instrument is self-designed.

A further determining factor in selecting an instrument is its complexity. It is necessary to determine if any background information is required to complete the survey, that the instructions are easy to follow, and that the reading level is appropriate. Also it is important to determine the way in which the results are reported and how complicated they are to interpret. Since all of these factors can influence the success of the remainder of the process, they should be given careful attention.

Administering the Survey. Prior to administering the survey, the participants should be informed of the purpose of the survey, how the data will be used, and how and when feedback of the results will be made available. Then, the survey is administered to all members of the college or, for more limited use, to a subsystem of the institution such as all those who report to the dean or vice-president of student affairs.

The survey should be administered in such a way that as close to 100 percent participation as possible is obtained. One possibility is to administer it at a time when all participants are a captive audience, such as at a staff or faculty meeting. Another possibility is coding the instruments so that those persons who did not complete one can be sent reminders. Regardless of the method used, however, the participants should be assured that their responses will be totally anonymous. Having the completed surveys sent to a neutral party,

98

perhaps the resource person or consultant, will further assure anonymity.

Feedback Sessions. In general, the results of the survey are fed back in functional work groups. French and Bell (1978) suggest that the first work group to receive the results be that of the chief executive officer. But, before the group sees the data, a resource person should help the work group leader alone interpret the data and also prepare him or her to lead the work group feedback meeting. The work group leader then shares the data with his or her team, with the resource person in attendance to help facilitate the process. During the meeting, the results of the survey are analyzed and discussed with special attention paid to those areas where discrepancies exist between present conditions and desired conditions. Finally, based on their analysis, the group proceeds to devise constructive plans to reduce those discrepancies.

The feedback session is the single most important element in the survey feedback process. Without it, of course, there would be no change, growth, or improvement. So, in view of its critical nature, there are a few considerations to keep in mind. The climate created for the meetings must be positive in order to promote trust and openness among the group members. The sessions should ideally take place when there will be no interruptions such as telephone calls. If there is no good place on campus, then consider having the meetings at an off-campus location. Whatever the circumstances, the feedback meeting must be clearly planned, organized, and orchestrated.

The final task for the work group during the feedback/planning session is to make plans for introducing the data to the next lower level of work groups. The team members then become the leaders of the work groups at that next level, and they repeat the feedback/planning process with that work group. The process continues in that manner until all levels who participated in the survey have gone through a feedback/planning session.

To illustrate, the first feedback session is held with the community college president and those who answer directly to him or her, such as vice-presidents or deans. When their session is finished, the dean of instruction becomes the leader for his or her work group, which might be made up of division chairpersons. They then have a feedback/planning session and make plans to share the data with the next lower level. The division chairpersons who are team members become team leaders for work groups that might consist of department chairpersons. As stated above, the same process continues until all levels have participated in a feedback session.

Follow-up. Someone in the institution should be made responsible for making sure that the action plans developed in the feedback sessions are carried out. This should be done during the early stages of planning the entire survey feedback process so that follow-up becomes an integral part of the process.

Effective follow-up should be conducted in two different ways. The first assumes that time lines are a part of each set of action plans. If so, the activities can be monitored for progress on or shortly after the time specified in the plan. The second type of follow-up activity should be a readministration of the original survey to determine if the desired changes actually took place. This becomes somewhat of a pre/post assessment activity and can be readministered more than once. The essence, then, of the follow-up activities is to determine first if the action plans have been carried out and second, if they have had the desired effect.

Available Survey Instruments

There is a wide variety of surveys, questionnaires, and instruments available for diagnosing and analyzing various aspects of the organization. A few of them are geared and written especially for use in the community college, some can be used in the community college exactly as they are written, and the remainder have to be adapted to eliminate, for example, language that is most frequently used only in business settings. Many of the surveys focus on specific topics or concerns such as those discussed earlier in this chapter. Others, especially those that deal with assessing organizational climate, contain indices that cover several of those topics.

There is, however, another broad category of surveys and instruments available that touch on some of the same concerns and topics that occur in OD, but they are best used in groups in which the focus is on individual learning and insight. The results of such surveys are frequently seen only by the individual and are not group-tabulated. There is, therefore, no group feedback, and planned change is not usually a part of the group outcomes.

The sources listed below are grouped into those that contain surveys that are designed specifically for the community college, those that contain surveys that are appropriate for the community college with little or no modification, those books or companies that offer multiple instruments, and those packaged approaches that have the surveys and meetings preplanned and programmed.

Community College Oriented Surveys

1. *Organizational Development Questionnaire*
   Source: Hadley, O. B., and Andrews, J. "The Development of a Questionnaire for an Organizational Development Program at Los Angeles Southwest College." (ED167 219).
   This questionnaire, containing 79 items, measures attitudes in several OD concept areas—institutional climate, supervisory relations, work departments relations, the job setting, institutional processes and results, and goal setting.

2. *Survey of Community college Organizational Functioning*
   Source: Mink, O. G. Graduate Program in Human Resource Development, EDB 406, The University of Texas at Austin, Austin, Texas 78712.
   The focus of this survey is organizational climate. It is an adaptation of the survey of organizations that was developed by the Institution of Social Research. It is based on Likert's System 4 model of organizational effectiveness.

3. *Organizational Growth Stages*
   Source: Mink, O. G. Graduate Program in Human Resource Development, EDB 406, The University of Texas at Austin, Austin, Texas 78712.
   Based on an original survey from Gordon Lippitt's Organizational Renewal materials, this survey helps institutions identify what stage of organizational growth they are in with respect to several key areas of concern, such as physical and financial resources, innovation and creativity, productivity, and social responsibility.

Surveys Appropriate for Community Colleges

1. *TORI Group Self-Diagnosis Scale*
   Source: Jones, J. E., and Pfeiffer, J. W. *1977 Annual Handbook for Group Facilitators.* San Diego: University Associates, 1977.
   The theory behind this survey is that trust is a determinant of effectiveness and productivity in groups. The survey provides scales for four levels of trust: trust, openness, realization, and interdependence. Ample suggestions for using the scale are provided.

2. *Group Effectiveness Survey*
   Source: Nadler, D. A. *Feedback and Organization Development: Using Data-Based Methods.* Reading, Mass.: Addison-Wesley, 1977.
   This survey focuses on the functioning of work groups. Indices include group task and composition, how group members work together, group effectiveness, and strengths and weaknesses of the group.

3. *Group Expectation Survey*
   Source: Bergquist, W. H., and Phillips, S. R. *A Handbook for Faculty Development, Vol. I.* Washington, D.C.: Council for Advancement of Small Colleges, 1975.
   Group norms are assessed in this survey so that groups can analyze the extent to which they share information about and reactions to group activities. It is also useful in analyzing expectations that individuals have of their own and others' group behavior.

4. *Diagnosing Organization Ideology*
   Source: Jones, J., and Pfeiffer, J. W. *1975 Annual Handbook for Group Facilitators.* San Diego: University Associates, 1975.
   This instrument is designed so that individuals can compare their patterns of behavior in an organization with the general pattern of behaviors that characterize an organization. Four orientations—power, role, task, and self—are assessed so that individuals can determine the fit between their values and those of the organization.

5. *Organizational Climate Questionnaire*
   Source: Litwin, G., and Stringer, R. Jr. *Motivation and Organizational Climate.* Boston: Division of Research, Graduate School of Business Administration, Harvard University, 1968.
   This survey assessing organizational climate has nine indices: structure, responsibility, rewards, risk, warmth, support, standards, conflict, and identity.

6. *Profile of Organizational Characteristics*
   Source: Foundation for Research on Human Behavior, Ann Arbor, Michigan.

7. *Survey of Organizations*
   Source: San Diego: University Associates.

The *Profile* was the original survey developed by the Institute for Social Research in 1946. The *Survey of Organizations* is the revised and improved version developed by David Bowers. Both are based on Likert's System 4 model of organizational development. An added feature of this survey is that it was designed specifically for use in a survey feedback intervention.

8. *Evaluating Your Organization*
   Source: Organizational Renewal, Inc., 5605 Lamar Road, Washington, D.C. 20016.
   This is the survey from which the Organizational Growth Stages survey by Mink was adapted.

9. *Organizational Climate Description Questionnaire*
   Source: Halpin, A. *Theory and Research in Administration.* Toronto, Canada: MacMillan, 1966.
   This survey on organizational climate has eight main variables: disengagement, hindrance, esprit, intimacy, aloofness, production, trust, and consideration.

Companies or Books Providing Surveys

1. Fox, R. S., et al. *Diagnosing Professional Climates of Schools.* Fairfax, Va.: NTL Learning Resources Corporation, 1975.
   Although it is designed for a public school audience, this book does provide a large number of climate-oriented surveys that could be adapted to the community college.

2. Francis, D., and Young, D. *Improving Work Groups: A Practical Manual for Team Building.* San Diego: University Associates, 1979.
   This book contains a variety of instruments that can be used in twelve different areas of team development such as appropriate leadership, commitment to the team, effective work methods, and positive intergroup relations. While some would need to be modified for community college use, many could be used without modification. Instructions are provided for the best utilization of the instruments.

3. Pfeiffer, J. W., Heslin, R., and Jones, J. E. *Instrumentation in Human Relations Training.* San Diego: University Associates, 1976.

This handy compendium contains at least forty instruments on organizational climate, leadership/management styles, supervisor-subordinate relations, and group dynamics. The authors provide a description of each survey together with information on administering, scoring, and interpreting the instrument.

Packaged Approaches

1. *Grid Organization Development*
   Source: Blake, R., and Mouton, J. *Building a Dynamic Corporation Through Grid Organization Development.* Reading, Mass.: Addison-Wesley, 1969.
   This approach has as its basis the managerial grid—a matrix for assessing leadership style. The program has six phases designed to train managers at all levels of the organization.

2. *ITORP—Implementing the Organizational Renewal Process*
   Source: Lippitt. G. Organizational Renewal, Inc., 5605 Lamar Road, Washington, D.C. 20016.
   ITORP is a five-phase program complete with numerous surveys and group meetings designed in general to improve organizational effectiveness.

Conclusions

In an earlier chapter, Woodman and Muse point out that survey feedback may be the single most frequently used OD intervention. This is a view shared by others, including Nadler (1977) and French and Bell (1978, p. 156), who conclude that ". . . survey feedback is a cost-effective means of implementing a comprehensive program, thus making it a highly desirable change technique."

Cost-effectiveness, however, is not the only reason for the popularity of survey feedback. Greiner (1967), in comparing eighteen studies of organization change efforts, found three features that were common to those efforts judged as successful. They were a strong need for change to occur, the involvement of many organizational levels in planning change, and shared decision making regarding change as opposed to unilateral or delegated decision making. All of these features, but especially the last two, are characteristic of survey feedback and would seem to indicate its utility. Further, Nadler (1977) points out that the use of a data-based intervention such as survey feedback influences the behavior change process in two main ways. First, it energizes behavior by arousing feelings and forces that create an impetus for change. Then, once the impetus is created, the data analysis helps to direct behavior by indicating those areas in which change should take place. So, the combination of data, data feedback, analysis, problem solving, and planning found in survey feedback creates a powerful force for change.

From the discussions above and the available research, it is apparent that survey feedback, if properly used, has the potential for being one of the most influential OD activities in which a community college can participate. Any community college that is seriously interested in improving its effectiveness and overall organizational fuctioning should give survey feedback serious consideration.

References

Anderson, B. R. "Communication Questionnaire." Unpublished dissertation, University of Arkansas, 1981.

Bell, C. R., and Nadler, L. (Eds.). *The Client-Consultant Handbook*. Houston: Gulf Publishing, 1979.

Bowers, D. G. "OD Techniques and Their Results in Twenty-three Organizations. The Michigan ICL Study." *The Journal of Applied Behavioral Science*, 1973, *9* (1), 21–43.

Bowers, D. G., and Franklin, J. L. *Data-Based Organizational Change*. San Diego: University Associates, 1977.

Fordyce, J. K., and Weil, R. *Managing with People—A Manager's Handbook of Organization Development Methods*. Reading, Mass: Addison-Wesley, 1971.

French, W. L., and Bell, C. H., Jr. *Organization Development: Behavioral Sciences Interventions for Organization Improvement*. (2nd ed.) Englewood Cliffs, N.J.: Prentice-Hall, 1979.

Friedlander, F., and Brown, L. D. "Organization Development." *Annual Review of Psychology*, 1974.

Greiner, L. E. "Patterns of Organizational Change." *Harvard Business Review*, 1967, *45*, 119–30.

Hadley, O. B., and Andrews, J. "The Development of a Questionnaire for an Organizational Development Program at Los Angeles Southwest College." Unpublished doctoral practicum, Nova University, 1978. (ED167 219).

Hammons, J. O., and Hunter, W. "Using Consultants to Improve Instruction." In J. O. Hammons (Ed.), *New Directions for Community Colleges*, no. 17. San Francisco: Jossey-Bass, 1977.

Likert, R. *The Human Organization*. New York: McGraw-Hill, 1967. *Management Development and Training Program for Colleges and Universities*. Coconut Grove, Fla.: Higher Education Management Institute, Inc., 1978.

Nadler, D. *Feedback and Organization Development: Using Data-Based Methods*. Reading, Mass.: Addison-Wesley, 1977.

Pfeiffer, J. W., Heslin, R., and Jones, J. E. *Instrumentation in Human Relations Training*. San Diego: University Associates, 1976.

Schmuck, R. A., and Miles, M. B. (Eds.). *Organization Development in Schools.* La Jolla, Calif.: University Associates, Inc., 1971.

Varney, G. H. *Organization Development for Managers.* Reading, Mass.: Addison-Wesley, 1977.

Gordon E. Watts is director of staff development at Westark Community College, Fort Smith, Arkansas, and an adjunct professor at the University of Arkansas. He is president-elect of the National Council for Staff, Program, and Organizational Development.

*How can one expect a consultant to accomplish
something a president is unwilling or unable
to do? The president should be the leader in
organization development.*

Organization Development:
A President's View

Byron N. McClenney

No other person in an institution of higher education has more
riding on the development of that institution than does the chief
executive. Selfish interests alone should be enough to compel a
person to do everything possible to produce positive developments.
If a person believes deeply in the mission of the institution, then he
or she works with heightened motivation to create a healthy
organization.

The Big Picture

There are some key characteristics of healthy organizations
that should be pursued by a president who wishes to produce positive developments. These desirable characteristics are as follows.

1. *A clear sense of mission.* This is a prerequisite for efforts to
develop an organization.

2. *Goal orientation.* A sense of priority about the ends toward which an organization works is crucial.

3. *Climate of trust.* Absence of this characteristic will
shortcircuit even the most creative plans for organization
development.

J. Hammons (Ed.) *New Directions for Community Colleges: Organization
Development—Change Strategies,* no. 37. San Francisco: Jossey-Bass, March 1982.

108

4. *Expectations of excellence.* Who wants to work for an organization without standards and self-respect? High expectations for individual and group performance provide a springboard for organization development.

5. *Collaborative relationships.* Units of the organization recognize the interdependence required to achieve efficiency and effectiveness for the total organization.

6. *Recognition of realities.* Healthy organizations continually assess the environment and face the difficult choices required in order to avoid stagnation or retrenchment.

The significance of leadership behavior, the needs of persons, the analysis of the forces at work in any situation, and assessment of the risks in proposed courses of action can now be discussed in terms of how to produce desirable outcomes.

Leadership for Organization Development

A president cannot escape the fact that he or she sets the tone for the way work is accomplished in the organization. A tone or climate is established by the way a president plans, organizes, directs, coordinates, and controls institutional processes. A healthy organization will result in proportion to the extent to which a leader is able to provide for the participation of people at all levels of the organization. People support the things they help to create, and a president who feels the need to tightly control all processes is missing an opportunity to unleash a positive force within the organization. Delegation of responsibility and authority, a willingness to provide for open and honest problem solving and decision making, and open communication help create the climate or atmosphere in which positive organization development can take place.

Needs of people

Whether one talks about students, faculty, staff or administrators, there are some common needs of people which should be kept in mind by those who hope to develop an organization. Common needs are: (1) to feel important, (2) to be respected, (3) to be informed, (4) to receive recognition and rewards, (5) to know the expectations held for performance, and (6) to have influence. Failure to recognize these common needs will lead to failure in efforts to initiate positive changes in the organization.

What a leader assumes about people also will have a significant impact. If the administrator assumes that people are basically lazy, then he or she is more likely to assume a very directive posture in most processes. Conversely, if the administrator assumes that people are basically purposive, then he or she is more likely to favor participative practices. Participative practices are more likely to create the conditions conducive for positive organization development.

Educators should be among the first leaders to recognize that positive feedback and rewards are better than punishment and sanctions as motivators for improved performance. Recognition of that belief will lead to a balance between accomplishment of goals and the needs of people. People must be seen as the keys to achieving purposes if one hopes to see personnel share a commitment to help the organization accomplish its purposes.

The Situation

There is a tendency among many in higher education to think about improving people through staff development or management development when there is a perceived need to improve an organization. Others place great faith in systems and forget about the needs of people. What is needed is an understanding regarding the interrelationship of people and structures in a specific situation. A good strategy for organization development in one setting might have a negative impact in another setting.

Basic to effective organization development is an understanding of the following:
1. Structural problems produce many behavioral problems.
2. Structural changes may lead to additional behavioral problems like resistance to change or frustration.
3. Many behavioral problems resulting from personal problems, lack of skills, and personality conflicts are not related to structural problems.
4. Behavioral changes without attention to underlying structural problems may lead to frustration.

Selection of an approach to changing structures or people, or both, must be based on a careful analysis of the needs of people and the organization. The process chosen through which to make a change, based in large measure on leadership style will be crucial.

As has been suggested, people want to be involved in determining changes with a major impact on their work. Recognition of the need for skill building and involvement in the processes leading to structural changes help people accept and contribute to positive change in an organization. In other words, the right structural change can be made through the wrong process and produce serious behavioral problems. On the other hand, the right process can lead to positive behavioral changes while at the same time solving structural problems.

Critical Structures

There are a number of structural elements which must be clear, reasonable, and understood by all persons in the organization if organization development is to reach its potential. Among the most important elements are:

1. *Role of individuals and groups in governance:* Who shall be involved in decision making and how shall they be involved? Who has authority to make committee appointments? Who makes final decisions?

2. *Performance review evaluation:* How shall performance be judged? For what purposes is evaluation undertaken? Who shall be involved in assessing performance?

3. *Position descriptions:* Do people have a clear understanding of their roles in the organization?

4. *Salary schedules classification structure:* How are levels of compensation to be determined? How are positions to be categorized and related to each other?

5. *Grievance procedures:* How are differences between people to be resolved? Is a peer committee to be involved?

6. *Promotion review:* What criteria are to be utilized? Who shall be involved in the review?

7. *Leave policies:* Under what circumstances can one be absent from assigned duties? Who shall approve requests for leave?

8. *Salary administration:* How are salary increases to be distributed? Is merit to have a place in the determination?

9. *Selection of personnel:* Who is to be involved? What is the role of affirmative action?

10. *Budgeting:* Who is to be involved: How are priorities established?

The list could be expanded, but the point is not to create an exhaustive list. These structural elements are examples of areas in which many institutions have problems that create barriers to organization development. Some problems can be solved by helping administrators develop or sharpen skills, some can be alleviated by involving the right people in a process to create a new policy, and others will require a combination of strategies. Awareness of the problems and the ability to attach a measure of importance to them is critical for a person desiring to provide leadership for organization development.

Assessment

The need facing a leader is to accurately assess the forces, whether political or structural, and determine the appropriate action or actions to stimulate positive development of the organization. Implicit in that thought is the notion that clarity exists regarding the mission and goals of the organization. Assessment of the extent to which clarity exists may be determined through surveys, the work of a task force, a series of hearings, or some other technique, but it is important to know if there is a collective vision of desirable directions for the future of the institution. Further, it is important to obtain feedback from various constituent groups and potential students. Again, surveys, advisory committees, and hearings can be useful in discovering gaps in service or evidence of dissatisfaction.

Given an understanding of how people perceive the organization, it is possible to begin a process of identifying the barriers or problems which seem to prevent positive development of the institution. For example, if the institution does not have clearly stated and understood policies and procedures, and people see that as a problem, then it will be important to address development of policies and procedures as a part of the effort to develop the organization. On another front, if supervisors do not know how to conduct the process of performance review, then workshops or seminars may be needed to equip them for what should be a process to help individuals improve performance.

Since presidents often hear only what others think they want to hear, the element of assessment is critical if the president is to have the information he or she needs to lead organization development. There are times when it might be most productive to bring an outside agent or consultant into the process to provide an objective view. In fact, evaluation teams from the regional accrediting associations can fill the role if they are allowed to and if their advice and observations are utilized in a forward-looking program to improve the institution. All too often, however, administrators get defensive and fail to reap the potential benefits. The point is, every organization can be better if it assesses its current status and develops an approach to move towards a higher level of operation. The president needs to lead the effort to formulate the plan for institutional improvement.

Setting the Example

Using his or her knowledge of the current status, a president who wants to provide leadership for development will do a checkup on the extent to which he or she is providing the example for good management. The president should, in fact, be in the lead role in answering the following questions: (1) What are we aiming to accomplish? (2) How shall we function? (3) Who will do the work? (4) Who must be kept informed? (5) How shall we evaluate results? These questions focus on the functions of planning, organizing, directing, coordinating, and controlling that are so vital if an organization is to be healthy. Planning, in particular, offers an opportunity on an annual basis to assess the status, create plans, and then allocate resources to encourage timely problem solving and new approaches to providing services.

If people in the organization can profit from skill building in areas like time management, conducting meetings, and team building, then a president would be wise to provide the learning opportunities. He or she cannot escape the need, however, to set an example. A president who demonstrates a willingness to learn new skills can inspire others to improve. A president also needs to recognize the hazard of sending a staff member to a workshop to get inspired to try something new when the organization has not been prepared to absorb the new approach.

The president in essence, must constantly see the "big picture," initiate action, coordinate structural changes and staff or management development programs, and communicate in an open fashion so that people understand the changes taking place in the organization. In effect, the president should manage the change process.

Summary

The president has primary responsibility for creating the climate or tone within the organization. He or she would do well to understand the impact of leadership style. It is also important to work constantly to understand the needs of the people who do the work of the organization. Assessing the forces in the environment of the institution should provide a foundation for determining needed changes and weighing the risks. Causing positive things to happen is the task, and involving people in the process is the way to achieve positive outcomes.

Byron N. McClenney is President of the Colleges, San Antonio Community College District, San Antonio, Texas.

*Additional references on organization
development from the ERIC Clearinghouse
on Junior Colleges.*

Sources and Information: Organization Development in the Community College

*Anita Colby
James C. Palmer*

This concluding chapter provides an annotated bibliography of recent ERIC documents and journal articles dealing with organization development in educational settings. The ERIC documents included in the bibliography were selected from additions to the ERIC database since 1976. Because of the greater volume of journal literature, only articles written in the past two years were considered for inclusion. While the literature on organization development is expanding, the number of articles and documents dealing specifically with two-year colleges remains relatively small. The articles and papers included in this bibliography do not all deal directly with the community college; however, all were selected because of their relevance and applicability to the two-year college setting.

The bibliography is organized in seven sections. The first of these cites additional sources of information about organization development theory and the conditions that are requisite for OD success. The second section deals with specific organization devel-

J. Hammons (Ed.) *New Directions for Community Colleges: Organization
Development—Change Strategies,* no. 37. San Francisco: Jossey-Bass, March 1982.

opment techniques and their application in educational settings. The third section cites documents and articles focusing on the role, training, and activities of the organizational development consultant. The fourth section provides citations to materials dealing with the application of organization development theory to staff and management development programs. Methods of evaluating OD efforts are covered in the fifth section, while the next section presents numerous case studies of the application of organization development programs and interventions in postsecondary institutions and departments. Finally, several resources that may be used in planning or implementing organization development programs are cited.

The ERIC documents (ED numbers) listed here, unless otherwise indicated, are available on microfiche or in paper copy from the ERIC Document Reproduction Service (EDRS), Computer Microfilm International Corporation, P.O. Box 190, Arlington, VA 22210. The microfiche price for documents under 481 pages is $0.91. Prices for paper copies are: 1-25 pages, $2.00; 26-50 pages, $3.65; 51–75 pages, $5.30; and 76–100 pages $6.95; for each additional 25 pages add $1.65. These prices are subject to change. Postage must be added to all orders. Abstracts of these and other documents in the junior college collection are available upon request from the ERIC Clearinghouse for Junior Colleges, 96 Powell Library, University of California, Los Angeles, CA 90024.

**Organization Development Theory
and General Information**

Baldridge, J.V. (Ed.), and Deal, T. E. (Ed.). *Managing Change in Educational Organizations: Sociological Perspectives, Strategies, and Case Studies.* Berkeley, Calif.: McCutchan Publishing Corp., 1975. (Available from McCutchan Publishing Corporation, 2526 Grove Street, Berkeley, Calif. 94704, $13.75).

Presents twenty-six articles that draw from social science research to investigate change processes in educational organizations at all levels. Major themes include organizational subsystems and processes involved in innovation, strategies that can be used to foster change in educational organizations, and the dynamics of educational change as revealed in case study analyses.

Bennis, W., and Jamieson, D. "Organization Development at the Crossroads." *Training and Development Journal,* April 1981, *35* (4), 18–26.

Examines the current state of organization development in terms of applications, unresolved problems, and OD's probable future role.

Collin, W. J. "Staff Development: An Organizational Skill for Survival." Paper presented at the International Institute on the Community College, Sarnia, Ontario, Canada, June 1978. 35 pp. (ED 172 866).
Defines staff development in terms of institutional renewal theory and presents a model for planning, organizing, and analyzing staff development activities, programs, and processes in the community colleges. Reviews the literature on staff and organizational development.

Cope, R. "Toward a Natural Systems Theory of Organizational Effectiveness: Integrating Geopolitical, Darwinistic and Strategic Planning Perspectives." Paper presented at the Annual Meeting of the Association for the Study of Higher Education, Washington D.C., March 1981. 28 pp. (ED 203 803).
Proposes a theory of organizational development based on turn-of-the-century geopolitical studies and reviews the work of current organizational theorists to identify six strategic characteristics of effective organizations. Three of these pertain to competitive advantage and three to the capacity to adapt.

Goddu, R. *Framework for Analysis and Insightful Action in Organizations.* Durham, N. H.: New England Program in Teacher Education, 1975. 8 pp. (ED 114 370).
Defines stages of organization development as a means of providing a framework within which individuals can assess where an organization is, what might be happening to it next, and what actions can be taken to influence its future development.

Jones, J. E., and others. "OD in the Eighties: Preliminary Projections and Comparisons." *Group and Organization Studies,* March 1980, 5 (1), 5-17.
Examines preliminary results of a Delphi study conducted to predict trends and problems in the field of organization development during the 1980s. Compares results with data from a group of OD practitioners.

Jung, C. C. *Organizational Development in Education. Preparing Educational Training Consultants: Organizational Development (PETC-III)*. Portland, Ore.: Northwest Regional Educational Lab, 1977. 263 pp. (ED 144 191—available in microfiche only).

Provides the theoretical framework for the PETC III program, an instructional system for training school system organizational development consultants. More specifically, presents a framework for the application of organization development in educational settings.

Kur, C. E. "OD: Perspectives, Processes and Prospects." *Training and Development Journal*, April 1981, *35* (4) 28–30, 32–34.

Reviews the history of organization development since 1969 and describes the emerging values and historical perspectives of the field. Provides a cross-section of processes and theories and clarifies the changing relationship between organization development and human resource development.

A Procedure for Strengthening Organizational Effectiveness. Cleveland, Ohio: Midwest Organization Development Network, 1974. 18 pp. (ED 119 342).

Provides a general introduction to organization development. Includes a 12-step process for beginning an OD program, an outline of seven major assumptions about organizations, an examination of the professional OD specialist, and a description of the Midwest Organization Development Network.

Rowan, H. "Some Key Factors in Policy Implementation." Paper presented at the Annual Meeting of the American Educational Research Association, San Francisco, Calif., April 19–23, 1976. 16 pp. (ED 122 381).

Examines organizational factors that affect policy implementation in public agencies, including the organization's mission, the degree of consensus on actions taken by the organization, the limitations imposed by external agencies, and the incentives of individuals working within the organization.

Warrick, D. D. "Managing the Stress of Organizational Development." *Training and Development Journal*, April 1981, *34* (4), 36–41.

Emphasizes the importance of recognizing and managing the stress produced by organization development and encourages practitioners to acknowledge stress management as an important organization development skill.

Organization Development Techniques and Applications

Arter, M. H. "Use of the Community College Goals Inventory (CCGI) as an Impetus for Change in a Rural Community College." Paper presented at the Annual Conference of the California Association of Institutional Research, San Francisco, Calif., February 1981. 23 pp. (ED 198 861).

Describes the efforts of Palo Verde College in California to establish priorities for long- and short-range planning based on the results of a survey of college faculty and administrators, community members, trustees, and students. Reports on areas where the CCGI revealed discrepancies between existing and ideal conditions.

Beatty, P. T. "A Case for Instructional Improvement Programs in Community Services." *Community College Review,* Fall 1980, *8* (2), 45–49.

Addresses questions to deans of community services related to faculty, instructional, and organizational development. Recommends eleven strategies for improving instruction through faculty orientations, faculty task forces, teacher resource centers, faculty survival guides, student service centers, mission and management councils, division newsletters, annual commencements, and small grant funds.

Blaesser, W. W. "Organization Change Strategies to Facilitate Student Development Models." Paper presented at the Annual Meeting of the American College Personnel Association, Chicago, Ill., April 1976. 21 pp. (ED 131 367).

Discusses how the principles and practices of organizational development can be successfully applied to the student development situation. Traces the history of such an approach.

Derr, C. B. *Major Causes of Organizational Conflict: Diagnosis for Action. Working Paper.* Monterey, Calif.: Naval Postgraduate School, 1975. 84 pp. (ED 120 906).

Examines factors that cause conflict within an organization and discusses alternative conflict management strategies. Details a paradigm to be used in selecting appropriate management strategies for differing conflict situations.

Dyer, W. G. "Selecting an Intervention for Organization Change." *Training and Development Journal,* April 1981, *35* (4), 62–66, 68.
Discusses the process of selecting an appropriate intervention strategy following an organizational diagnosis.

Hadley, O. B., and Andrews, J. "The Development of a Questionnaire for an Organizational Development Program at Los Angeles Southwest College." Ed. D. Practicum, Nova University, 1978. 45 pp. (ED 167 219).
Describes the creation of an organizational development questionnaire covering institutional climate; supervisory, work department, job, and institutional process indices; institutional results; and goal-setting comparisons between current and ideal situations. Includes a questionnaire, bibliography, and literature review on organization development.

Herzog, E. L. "Improving Productivity via Organization Development." *Training and Development Journal,* April 1980, *34* (4), 36–39.
Details a six-part process for productivity improvement through OD intervention, covering awareness of needs, entry of specialist, data collection, problem identification, action planning, and implementation of solutions.

Lindquist, J. *Strategies for Change.* Berkeley, Calif.: Pacific Soundings Press, 1978. (ED 200 113—available in microfiche only).
Offers strategies for change in higher education in sections covering: planned change theory and research, case histories of planned change, and innovation as an adaptive development. Includes bibliographies.

Martorana, S. V., and Kuhns, E. "Analyzing a Force for Change: Discrepancy between Aspiration and Achievement of Institutional Goals." Paper presented at the Annual Association of Institutional Research Forum, Houston, Texas, 1978. 18 pp. (ED 161 336).
Analyzes the discrepancy between aspiration and achievement of institutional goals as an important variable in monitoring the life cycle of an innovation through exploration to institutionali-

133

J

Jamieson, D., 116–117
Job redesign: in community colleges, 41; shift to, 29; subsystem effects of, 32, 39; trends in, 28–29
Jones, J. E., 100, 101, 102–103, 104, 117
Jones, J. P., 8
Jung C. C., 118

K

Kahn, R. L., 26, 43
Kanter, R. M., 38, 44
Kaplan, R. E., 34, 35, 43
Katz, D., 26, 43
Kaufman, S., 43
Kellogg Foundation, W. K., and National Institute for Staff and Organizational Development, 2, 72–73, 74, 75, 77, 78, 79, 81, 83, 85, 86, 90
Kest, D. L., 2, 19, 55–67
King, D. C., 37, 43, 125
Kozoll, C. E., 124
Kuhns, E., 120–121
Kur, C. E., 118
Kurpius, D. J., 122

L

Laboratory training, as organization development source, 8–9, 24–25
Lawler, E. E., 39, 43, 44
Lawrence, P. R., 27, 42
Levinson, H., 8
Lewin, K., 8, 9
Life-styles, and organizations, 47–49
Likert, R., 9, 60, 67, 93, 100, 102, 104
Lindquist, J., 76, 89, 120
Lippitt, G. L., 6, 21, 100, 103
Lippitt, R., 8
Lipshitz, R., 34, 43
Litwin, G., 101
Los Angeles Southwest College, survey instrument for, 97, 120
Lowman, R. L., 122–123
Luke, R. A., 38, 43

M

McClenney, B. N., 3, 107–113
McGarry, N. S., 127

McGregor, D., 8
McIntyre, M., 127
Management, effective, characteristics of, 57–58
Management development: organization development distinct from, 9–10; sources on, 123–125
Mann, F. C., 79, 90
Margulies, N., 52, 54
Martorana, S. V., 120–121
Matrix of organizations, shift to, 27–28
Mechanistic systems, shift from, 26–27
Media Systems Corporation, and National Institute for Staff and Organizational Development, 74–75, 84
Michigan, University of, Survey Research Center (SRC) at, 9
Michigan State University, Office of Health Services Education and Research at, 127–128
Midwest Organization Development Network, 118
Miles, M. B., 18, 21, 91–92, 105
Miller, E. C., 31, 38, 43
Mink, O. G., 80, 90, 100
Mintzberg, H., 69, 70, 78, 90
Mirvis, P. H., 43
Mitchell, T., 31, 44
Monitoring, stage of, 16
Montagna, P. D., 70, 90
Moore, D. E., Jr., 124
Mouton, J. S., 7, 9, 11, 13, 16, 17–18, 19, 20, 31, 42, 71, 90, 103
Muse, W. V., 1, 23–44, 103

N

Nadler, D. A., 26, 38, 43, 91, 95, 101, 103, 104
Nadler, L., 96, 104
National Institute for Staff and Organizational Development (NISOD): Creative Teaching Series of, 83–84; described, 69–90; goals of, 73; impact of, 86–87; *Innovation Abstracts* of, 84–85; lessons from, 87–89; membership criteria for, 76–77; and network, 75–78; 88–89; as partnership, 72–75; products of, 83–85, 88; purpose of, 2, 74; strategies

134

NISOD (continued)
of, 78–83; Summer Institute of, 82–83, 89; and training, 85–86
National Training Laboratory, 8, 53
Needs assessment: in change strategy, 79–80; phase of, 60, 62; and survey feedback, 95

O

Objectives, use of, in management, 58
OD Network, 54
Office of Institutional Research and Planning (OIRP), 123
Organization development: in business, 23–44; case studies of, sources on, 126–128; as change strategy, 11–13; characteristics of professionals in, 51–52; and community colleges, 1, 40–42, 53–54, 69–70; conceptual base of, 8–9; consultants, sources on, 122–123; and criteria for professional status, 52; data and experience in, 12–13; defined, 5–7, 46, 92; demand for, 46–49; effectiveness of, 14–15; evaluation of, sources on, 125–126; evolution and trends of, 24–29; as fad, more than, 7–8; goal of, 39; and goal setting, 13; in higher education, 19; history of, 50–51; implementing, 15–16; ineffective, reasons for, 29–30; issues in, 45–54; laboratory training as source of, 8–9, 24–25; leadership for, 20, 108, 112; management development distinct from, 9–10; model for, 72; national effort toward, 55–67; need for, 109–110; outcomes of, 13–14; overview of, 5–21; partnership for, 69–90; and prerequisites, 16–18; president's view of, 107–113; problems in, 52–53; and professional status, 49–52; resources for, sources on, 128–130; results of change strategies in, 29–40; role of, 71–72; sources of information about, 20, 115–130; staff and, sources on, 123–125; strategies in, 18–19; structural elements in, 110–111; subsystem effects of, 31–40; survey feedback for, 9, 91–105; systems orientation of, 12; techniques and applications of, sources on,

119–121; theory of, sources on, 116–119; term of, 9
Organizations: assessment of, 111–112; characteristics desirable in, 107–108; collateral, 28, 38; effectiveness of, 56–57; life-styles in, 47–49; needs of people in, 108–109

P

Palmer, J. C., 115–130
Palo Verde College, survey at, 119
Partin, J. J., 51–52, 54
Pasmore, W. A., 27, 37, 43
Pecorella, P. A., 42
Pennsylvania State University, Planning Studies in Continuing Education Division of, 126
Pesuth, F. X., 127
Pfeiffer, J. W., 50, 54, 96, 97, 100, 101, 102–103, 104
Phillips, S. R., 101
Pickelman, J. E., 128
Pino, R. F., 129–130
Porras, J. I., 32, 44
Porter, L. W., 29, 44
Posner, B. Z., 121
Powell, G. N., 121
Preparing Educational Training Consultants (PETC-III), 118, 129–130
President: as example, 112; and organization development, 107–113
Price, R. D., 127–128
Priest, B. J., 128
Problem-solving process, concept of, 6
Process consultation, subsystem effects of, 32, 34–35
Providing Organizational Development Skills (PODS), 130

R

Randall, L. K., 8, 21
Randolph, W. A., 121
Raney, C., 69n
Renewal process, concept of, 6
Resource person, for survey feedback, 95–96
Rice, A., 27, 44
Roeber, R.J.C., 49, 54
Rogers, D., 121
Rose, C., 128

Roueche, J., 69*n*
Rowan, H., 118

S

St. John, E. P., 125-126
St. Petersburg Junior College, case study of, 127
Schaffer, R. H., 16-17, 21
Schein, E. H., 19, 21, 25, 34, 44
Schlesinger, L. E., 90
Schmidt, W. H., 9, 21
Schmuck, R. A., 18, 21, 91-92, 105
Scientific management, shift from, 28-29
Seashore, C. N., 90
Sensitivity training, shift from, 24-25
Shell United Kingdom, sociotechnical interventions by, 37
Shephard, H., 9, 51
Sherwood, J. J., 27, 34, 35, 36, 39, 43, 44, 125
Sikes, W. W., 80, 90
Sociotechnical interventions: in community colleges, 41; shift to, 26-27; subsystem effects of, 32, 37-38
Sorensen, J. E., 70, 90
Sorensen, T. L., 70, 90
Staff developer, in change strategy, 78-79, 88
Standards, in management, 58
Static organizational forms, shift from, 27-28
Steers, R. M., 56, 67
Stein, B. A., 38, 44
Strauss, G., 25, 44
Stringer, R., Jr., 101
Structural change, subsystem effects of, 32, 38
Summer, C., 90
Support, mutual, in management, 57
Survey feedback: advantages of, 93-94; analysis of, 91-105; in community colleges, 40-41; concepts of, 91-92; effective use of, 95-99; examples of items for, 93; feedback sessions for, 98-99; follow-up for, 99; instruments for, 96-97, 99-103; as organization development source, 9; potential of, 103-104; purpose for, 96; research on, 95; shift to, 26; shortcomings of, 94; subsystem effects of,

32, 36-37; survey administration for, 97-98

T

Tannenbaum, R., 24, 44
Tavistock Institute, and sociotechnical interventions, 37
Taylor, J. C., 39, 42
Team development: in community colleges, 40; shift to, 24-25; subsystem effects of, 32, 35-36
Teamwork, in management, 57
Texas Association for Community Service and Continuing Education, 83
Texas at Austin, University of: Community College Leadership Program of, 73; Institute on Staff Development and Conference of Presidents at, 82-83, 89; and National Institute for Staff and Organizational Development, 72, 74, 75, 76, 87; Program in Community College Education at, 74
Thompson, T. R., 71, 89
Tolchinsky, P. D., 28, 38, 44
Toomb, K., 121
Trist, E. L., 27, 44

U

U.S. Department of Labor, 54

V

Vaill, P. B., 51, 54
Van Wijk, A., 57, 58, 67
Variables, process and outcome, 32, 34
Varney, G. H., 2, 7, 9, 20, 21, 45-54, 91, 97, 105, 123

W

Walker, P. D., 121
Wallace, J., 52, 54
Walton, R., 19, 21, 34, 44
Ward, W., 130
Warrick, D. D., 118-119
Watkins, K., 69*n*
Watts, G., 3, 91-105
Weathersby, G. B., 125-126
Webber, R., 90

136

Weil, R., 95, 104
Western Electric, Hawthorne studies
  at, 26
Whitcomb, D. B., 125
White, S., 31, 44
Windsor, University of, case study of,
  126
Woodman, R. W., 1, 23–44, 103
Work team, concept of, 6
Workshops, in change strategy, 81–82,
  88–89

Y

Young, D., 102

Z

Zand, D. E., 28, 44
Zawacki, R. A., 43
Zenger, J. H., 9, 10, 21
Zimmer, F. G., 26, 42

132

Cuyahoga Community College, case study of, 126-127

D

Dallas County Community College District, case study at, 128
Davey, J. M., 43
Davis, L. E., 39, 42
Davis, S. A., 24, 44
Davis, S. M., 27, 42
Deal, T. E., 116
Decision making, in management, 57
Derr, C. B., 119-120
Diagnosis: intervention linked with, 30-31; stage of, 15-16
DiCarlo, R. D., 126, 127
Dillon-Peterson, B., 123
Dyer, W. G., 25, 42, 120

E

Eadie, D. C., 126-127
Educational Testing Service, 40
Effectiveness, of organizations, 56-57
Ehly, S., 128
Eliason, M., 128
Ellison, N. M., 126-127
Emory, R. P., 129-130
ESSO, laboratory training at, 9
Evaluation: performance, in management, 58; sources on, 125-126; stage of, 16, 63-64
Exxon Education Foundation, and Higher Education Management Institute, 55, 56

F

Feedback. See Survey feedback
Florida Assessment and Diffusion System (FADS), 121
Ford, R. N., 39, 42
Fordyce, J. K., 95, 104
Foster, F., 69n
Fox, R. S., 102
Francis, D., 102
Franklin, J. L., 26, 42, 95, 104
French, W. L., 6, 7-8, 9, 12, 13, 15, 16, 18, 20, 21, 24, 25, 26, 43, 46, 54, 91, 92, 93, 95, 98, 103, 104
Friedlander, F., 15, 21, 34, 35, 36, 37, 43, 47, 48n, 54, 91, 95, 104
Fuller, S., 46, 54

Fund for the Improvement of Postsecondary Education, and National Institute for Staff and Organizational Development, 74, 83, 85

G

Gaff, J. G., 81, 90
Gall, J. P., 122
General Motors: need for organization development at, 46; organization development activities at, 31; parallel organization at, 38; sociotechnical interventions at, 37
Gibson, J., 67
Goddu, R., 117, 129
Golernbrowski, R. T., 54
Goodwin, N. L., 127
Greenfield Community College, case study of, 126, 127
Greiner, L. E., 103, 104

H

Hackman, F. R., 43
Hackman, J. F., 44
Hadley, O. B., 93, 97, 100, 104, 120
Halpin, A., 102
Hammons, J. O., 1-21, 92, 96, 104, 123-124
Hampton, D., 71, 72, 77, 78, 90
Harris, R. T., 49, 54
Harrison, R., 16, 18, 21, 36, 43
Herbst, R. G., 27, 43
Herzog, E. L., 120
Heslin, R., 102-103, 104
Higher Education Management Institute (HEMI), 124-125; accomplishments of, 64-65; described, 55-67; institutions in, 56, 66; program design of, 58-60; program phases of, 60-64; purpose of, 55; role of, 2; training in, 62-63
Hill, P., 37, 43
Hoffman, C. K., 129
Houston, W. R., 124
Hunter, W., 96, 104
Huse, E. F., 24, 27, 36, 37, 43, 51, 54

I

Initiative, and management, 57
Institutional Goals Inventory (IGI), 40-41

Index

A

Action planning, stage of, 16, 62
Action research, concept of, 7
Alderfer, C. P., 15, 20, 35, 38, 42
American Council on Education, 56
American Society of Training and
  Development, 5; Organization De-
  velopment Division of, 7, 20, 54
Anderson, B. R., 93, 104
Andrews, J., 93, 97, 100, 104, 120
Armes, N., 69n
Arter, M. H., 119
AT&T, job redesign at, 39
Attitude surveys, shift from, 26
Averch, V. R., 43

B

Baker, G. A., III, 2, 19, 69–90
Baldridge, J. V., 116
Barnette, J. J., 126
Barry, J. R., 125
Beatty, P. T., 119
Beck, L. L., 125
Beckhard, R., 12, 13, 20, 49, 54
Beer, M., 25, 30, 35, 37, 42
Bell, C. H., Jr., 6, 7–8, 9, 12, 13, 15, 16,
  18, 20, 21, 24, 26, 43, 46, 54, 91, 92, 93,
  95, 98, 103, 104
Bell, C. R., 96, 104
Bell, W., 122
Benne, K., 8
Bennis, W. G., 13, 20, 25, 44, 116–117
Berg, P. O., 32, 44
Bergquist, W., 76, 89, 101
Blaesser, W. W., 119
Blake, R. R., 7, 9, 11, 13, 16, 17–18, 19,
  20, 31, 42, 71, 90, 103
Block, P., 43
Booth, D., 126
Bowers, D. G., 26, 30, 31, 36, 42, 95,
  102, 104
Bradford, L., 8
Brown, L. D., 15, 21, 34, 35, 37, 43, 91,
  95, 104

Brown, P. J., 54
Burke, W. W., 9, 21

C

California, San Francisco, University
  of, School of Dentistry at, 128
Cammann, C., 122
Cammon, C., 43
Campbell, J. P., 56, 67
Campus development team (CDT), in
  change strategy, 80–81
Cass, E. L., 26, 42
Certified Consultants International
  (CCI), 50
Chamberlain, P. C., 122
Change: awareness of need for, 15; evo-
  lutionary and revolutionary, 11, 70;
  institutional, strategies for, 78–83
Change agent, concept of, 7
Chase, P. H., 7, 21
Cherns, A. B., 39, 42
Claxton, C. S., 123
Colby, A., 115–130
Collaborative management, concept
  of, 6
Collin, W. J., 117
Collins, R. W., 57, 67
Communication, in management, 57
Community College Goals Inventory
  (CCGI), 119
Community colleges: as dysfunc-
  tional, 70; Kellogg Consortium of,
  75, 78, 83, 84; organization devel-
  opment implications for, 40–42;
  organization development match
  with, 1, 53–54, 69–70; rationale for
  intervention in, 71; survey instru-
  ments for, 100–102
Comstock, V. N., 80, 90
Cope, R., 117
Cotton, C. C., 51, 54
Cresswell, A., 128
Cross, K. P., 71, 90
Culture, concept of, 6

131

Laboratory, 1977. 144 pp. (ED 144 192—available in microfiche only).

An instructional manual for use by senior trainers in charge of PETC-III programs. Outlines instructional strategies and includes samples of memos, work assignments, and additional resources.

Pino, R. F., and Emory, R. P. *Participant Materials. Preparing Educational Training Consultants: Organizational Development (PETC-III).* 410 pp. (ED 144 193—available in microfiche only).

Presents procedural guidelines, instructional materials, and relevant background information and theoretical data for use by the participants in the PETC-III program. Corresponds to the instructional strategies suggested in the trainers' manual (ED 144 192).

Ward, W., and others. *Providing Organizational Development Skills (PODS): A Combined Training Program.* Portland, Ore.: Northwest Regional Educational Laboratory, 1976. 221 pp. (ED 144 190).

Describes the PODS program, a series of eight instructional systems that together are intended to provide educators with the knowledge, skills, and sensitivities to organize and manage educational systems in a more relevant, humane, effective, and efficient way. Reviews organizational development theory, presents case studies, and proposes an implementation strategy.

Anita Colby is documents coordinator at the ERIC Clearinghouse for Junior Colleges, University of California at Los Angeles.

James Palmer is User Services Librarian at the ERIC Clearinghouse for Junior Colleges, University of California at Los Angeles.

Goddu, R. *Handbook for Supervision of Personnel in Performance Based Management Organizations.* Durham, N.H. New England Program in Teacher Education, 1975. 21 pp. (ED 111 790).

Provides rating scales, performance analysis forms, and other materials that can be used in specifying organization objectives, detailing the individual employee's role in supporting these objectives, and identifying performance evaluation criteria in terms of organization requirements. Discusses the use of these materials in negotiating written performance contracts between employees and supervisors.

Hoffman, C. K. *A Catalogue of Products That Can Aid Schools in Doing Organizational Development and Needs Assessment.* Tallahassee: Florida State Department of Education, 1979. 40 pp. (ED 181 561).

Reviews products and publications designed to help schools understand and become more skilled in group process, interpersonal communication, group problem solving, planning for change, and improving relationships in complex school organizations. Additionally, reviews needs assessment products and information. Annotations provide information on types of faculty activities, personnel requirements, time needs, expected outcomes, and sources of further information.

Organizational Development Workbook. Volume 1. Washington, D.C.: Aurora Associates, 1980. 174 pp. (ED 188 030).

Provides instructions and practice instruments for implementing four phases of organizational development: (1) initiation of the change process; (2) development of organizational change/intervention plans; (3) implementation of planned organization improvement; and (4) evaluation of the effort.

Organizational Development Workbook. Volume II. Washington, D.C.: Aurora Associates, 1980. 180 pp. (ED 188 031).

Presents a hypothetical example of the organizational development process designed to help the user understand the utility of the organizational development model.

Pino, R. F., and Emory, R. P. *Instructional Strategies. Preparing Educational Training Consultants: Organizational Development (PETC-III).* Portland, Oregon: Northwest Regional Educational

128

tions of planning, organization, coordination, monitoring, and assessing instructional development projects.

Priest, B. J., and Pickelman, J. E. *Increasing Productivity in the Community College: An Action-Oriented Approach.* Washington, D.C.: American Association of Community and Junior Colleges, 1976. 40 pp. (ED 125 721).

Defines and discusses the concept of educational productivity and describes the step-by-step procedure used at the Dallas County Community College District to identify ways of increasing cost-effectiveness.

Rose, C., and others. *Organizational Development Project U.C.S.F. School of Dentistry. Summary Report.* Los Angeles, Calif.: Evaluation and Training Institute, 1979. 10 pp. (ED 175 354).

Describes a two-part organizational development effort carried out at the School of Dentistry of the University of California, San Francisco. The needs assessment phase identified critical organizational and curricular problems, recommended appropriate points for intervention, and designed an ongoing program for planned change and institutional renewal. The second phase focused on defining curricular goals and objectives.

Resources

Cresswell, A., and others. *School Business Management Techniques: A Compendium.* Albany: New York State Association of School Business Officials; and Albany: State University of New York, 1980. 96 pp. (ED 182 826—available in microfiche only).

Describes approximately thirty management science and organizational behavioral techniques in terms of the mechanics of using the technique, specific applications, and requirements and constraints. Includes general management techniques, data analysis techniques, decision-making techniques, planning techniques, and management and organizational development techniques.

Ehly, S. and Eliason, M. "Organizational Development: A Collection of References from Education, Psychology, and Business." Unpublished bibliography, May 1980. 25 pp. (ED 190 940).

Bibliography focusing on organizational development in educational settings, and on organizational development theory and practical applications. Citations are not annotated.

127

and uniform college planning and management procedures. Major accomplishments are detailed and suggestions are provided.

Goodwin, N. L., and DiCarlo, R. D. *The Greenfield Plan: An Approach to Organizational Development.* Greenfield, Mass.: Greenfield Community College, 1979. 7 pp. (ED 196 493).
Describes Greenfield Community College's participatory management process, which incorporates a reorganized governance structure, data collection, a mechanism for establishing and implementing institutional goals, and an evaluation component.

McGarry, N. S. "Counselors and Faculty: Synthesis of Service for Holistic Education. A Community College Action Program for Organizational Development." Ed. D. Practicum, Nova University, 1975, 273 pp. (ED 138 901).
Discusses a community college action program in which a modified Delphi technique was used to create within faculty and counselors an awareness of the need to break down the artificial barriers between the two groups and to focus attention on the commonality of their perceptions and goals.

McIntyre, M. "Organization Development: A Case Study in Blockages." *Journal of Physical Education and Recreation,* March 1981, *52* (3), 71–74.
Examines standard procedures in organization development.

Pesuth, F. X. "A Survey of The Management System at St. Petersburg Junior College Using Likert's Profile." Ed. D. Practicum, Nova University, 1976. 47 pp. (ED 129 342).
Describes a study conducted at St. Petersburg Junior College of current perceptions and future expectations of organizational climate held by faculty, professional personnel, and upper-level management. Recommends a number of organizational development interventions to reduce the discrepancy among the groups.

Price, R. D. "Managing the Instructional Development Process." Paper presented at the Association for Educational Communications and Technology Annual Conference, Anaheim, California, 1976. 23 pp. (ED 125 529).
Describes the efforts of the Office of Health Services Education and Research at Michigan State University to clarify the func-

126

how a sequential pattern of development can be used to diag-
nose an institution's current state of development. Provides a
bibliography.

Case Studies

Barnette, J. J. "The Role of Evaluation in Organization Development. Evaluation in Support of the Pennsylvania ABE Improvement Program." Paper presented at the Annual Meeting of the
American Educational Research Association, New York, N.Y.,
April 1977. 22 pp. (ED 152 824—available in microfiche only).
    Defines organizational development and describes the con-
text, input, process, and product (CIPP) evaluation paradigm used
by the Planning Studies in Continuing Education Division of the
Pennsylvania State University in support of the organizational
development of the Pennsylvania Adult Basic Education Program.

Booth, D. *The Making of a Good Department. Structure and Process
in Departmental Development.* Paper presented at the Annual
Meeting of the Canadian Sociology and Anthropology Association, Edmonton, Alberta, Canada, 1978. 27 pp. (ED 203 821).
    Reviews the process used by the sociology department at the
University of Windsor, Ontario to resolve conflict and polarization
problems. Discusses the strategies used and the new departmental
structures developed.

DiCarlo, R. *Institutional Goals/Objectives for the Academic Year
1980-1981: Report of the Retreat/Planning Session (June 25-27,
1980).* Greenfield, Mass.: Greenfield Community College, 1980.
50 pp. (ED 196 495).
    Describes Greenfield's planning retreat, which involved
faculty, administration and staff in the development of institutional
goals and objectives. Includes results of the evaluation of the retreat
by participants.

Ellison, N. M., and Eadie, D. C. *The CCC Institutional Development Program: Organizational Change from the Chief Executive's Perspective.* Cleveland, Ohio: Cuyahoga Community College, 1978. 33 pp. (ED 179 256).
    Describes Cuyahoga Community College's three-phase insti-
tutional development program that sought to provide systematic

and evaluation. A bibliography, survey data, and sample modules are appended.

Whitcomb, D. B., and Beck, L. L. "Institutional Mission and Faculty Development." Paper presented at the Annual Meeting of the National Council for Social Studies, New Orleans, Louisiana, December 1980. 16 pp. (ED 195 198).

Considers faculty development in relation to student needs through instructional development, faculty needs through personal and professional development, and institutional needs through a focus on organizational development.

Evaluation of Organization Development

Barry, J. R. "Evaluating Organizational Consultation in a Changing World." Paper presented at the Annual Convention of the American Psychological Association, Montreal, Quebec, Canada, September 1980. 13 pp. (ED 198 437).

Suggests criteria for evaluating organizational consultation and identifies the factors which make these efforts difficult to assess. Discusses criteria including client satisfaction and participant flexibility.

King, D. C., and Sherwood, J. J. *Monitoring the Process and Evaluating the Results of Organization Development. Paper No. 452.* Lafayette, Ind.: Herman C. Krannert Graduate School of Industrial Administration, Purdue University, 1974. 28 pp. (ED 114 932).

Describes five alternatives for evaluating organization development projects. Examines advantages and disadvantages of each method and discusses obstacles presented by various parties to the evaluation effort.

St. John, E. P., and Weathersby, G. B. *Institutional Development in Higher Education: A Conceptual Framework for Evaluation: Appendix B. The Development of Institutions of Higher Education: Theory and Assessment of Impact of Four Possible Areas of Federal Intervention.* Cambridge, Mass.: Graduate School of Education, Harvard University, 1977. (ED 148 243).

Applies theories of economic and organizational development to the creation of a conceptual framework for the evaluation of the impact of institutional improvement programs. Suggests improved. Looks at ways of promoting change and factors that impede organizational development.

Houston, W. R. (Ed.), and others. *Staff Development and Educational Change.* Washington, D. C.: Association of Teacher Educators; and Omaha: Center for Urban Education, University of Nebraska, 1980. 156 pp. (ED 193 227—available in microfiche only).

Considers the long-range goals of staff development, the behaviors of participants, the interface of existing organizational structures, and the mechanisms for program planning and development.

Kozoll, C. E., and others. "Staff and Organizational Development: An Analysis of Their Interaction in a Community College Setting and Resulting Changes." Paper prepared for the Adult Education Research Conference, San Antonio, Texas, April 1978. 20 pp. (ED 152 989).

Describes a project undertaken by a university to develop in-service staff development programs for 500 part-time faculty members at three community colleges. The university project staff functioned as process consultants. A major project outcome was the recognition of the link between staff and organizational development.

Kozoll, C. E., and Moore, D. E., Jr. "Professional Growth vs. Fiscal Restraint." *Community College Frontiers,* Summer 1979, 7 (4), 18–22.

Keynotes the problems of organization and staff development programs during times of fiscal scarcity. Suggests a four-phase process to unify staff and organization development. Offers planning and evaluation criteria to facilitate decision making and consolidate money for high-impact programming.

Management Development and Training Program for Colleges and Universities. Program Handbook, May 1978. Coconut Grove, Fla.: Higher Education Management Institute, 1978. 93 pp. (ED 159 946).

Outlines the background and activities of a management training and development program implemented in five phases: introduction, needs assessment, action planning, implementation,

ing an assessment of the client's system; and (3) sharing a futuristic view of the organization. Recommends areas for consultant training.

Varney, G. H. "Developing OD Competencies." *Training and Development Journal*, April 1980, *34* (4), 30–35.
Defines the organization professional in terms of personal traits and requisite competencies. Outlines a learning sequence for OD skills development and presents a skills assessment scale for self-evaluation.

Staff and Management Development

Claxton, C. S. "Comprehensive Staff Development in the Community College: Implications for the Office of Institutional Research and Planning." Paper presented at the Annual Meeting of the American Educational Research Association, New York, N.Y., April 1977. 19 pp. (ED 136 857).
Outlines areas where the Office of Institutional Research and Planning (OIRP) can use its expertise in staff and organization development. Suggests that the OIRP serve as a key resource in assessing staff development needs, establishing program goals, and evaluating goal attainment.

Dillon-Peterson, B. (ED.), and others. *Staff Development/Organization Development*. Alexandria, Va.: Association for Supervision and Curriculum Development, 1981. 150 pp. (ED 196 919—available in microfiche only).
Covers in six chapters: (1) staff and organization development from a 1981 perspective, (2) staff development from the perspective of individual change, (3) organizational development as a tool for educational change, (4) models for designing effective staff development programs, (5) methods of evaluating staff development, and (6) a staff development scenario for the future.

Hammons, J. O. "Staff Development Is Not Enough." Paper presented at the Annual Meeting of the National Council of Staff, Program, and Organizational Development, Dallas, Texas, Summer 1978. 17 pp. (ED 194 144).
Argues that staff development activities that affect professional ability must be coupled with organizational development efforts if employee motivation and organizational climate are to be

122

Organizational Development Consultants

Bell, W., and others. *Report of the Annual Conference for Facilitators of Organizational Development in Education*, 2nd, Eugene, Oregon, February 1979. 40 pp. (ED 185 701).
Includes presentations and summaries of discussions at the conference.

Cammann, C. "Diagnosis and Change or Change and Diagnosis." Paper presented at the Annual Convention of the American Psychological Association, Montreal, Quebec, Canada, September 1980. 17 pp. (ED 201 947).
Recognizes a preparatory dimension to the work of organizational consultants, adding the preparation of organizations to conduct diagnosis and change to the traditional view of the consultant's role. Suggests conditions under which significant intervention and change are required before diagnosis can be conducted.

Chamberlain, P. C. "Improving Organizational Performance: The Key Variables for Institutions of Higher Education." *Improving Human Performance Quarterly*, Winter 1979, *8* (4), 234-41.
Details a set of variables to be considered by the change interventionist while working with higher education institutions.

Gall, J. P., and others. *Report of the Annual Conference for Facilitators of Organization Development in Education*, 3rd, Eugene, Oregon, January 31-February 2, 1980. 36 pp. (ED 185 702).
Describes the format and proceedings of the conference.

Kurpius, D. J. "OD; A Theory and Process for Influencing Human and Organization Development." *Improving Human Performance Quarterly*, Winter 1979, *8* (4), 217-26.
Offers a conceptual framework for organization development consultation in business and higher education settings.

Lowman, R. L. "Constructing Relationships from which to Change Organizations." Paper presented at the Annual Convention of the American Psychological Association, Montreal, Quebec, Canada, September 1980. 12 pp. (ED 201 937).
Provides suggestions for organizational consultants in their role as change agents for organizations. Identifies three primary tasks of consultation: (1) establishing a trust relationship; (2) mak-

zation. Explains the use of a magnitude estimation scaling as a step toward determining goal hiatus.

Powell, G. N., and Posner, B. Z. "Managing Change: Attitudes, Targets, Problems, and Strategies." *Group and Organization Studies*, September 1980, *5* (3), 310-23.

Details a model to be used by managers in selecting an appropriate change strategy following an educational diagnosis.

Randolph, W. A., and others. "An Experiential Design for Training in OD." *Training and Development Journal*, November 1979, *33* (11), 76-78, 80, 82-87.

Presents an organization training model that is eclectic, inexpensive, and applicable to participants with varying degrees of experience. Examines the design of an OD training laboratory.

Rogers, D. " 'General Systems Theory,' 'Modern Organizational Theory,' and Organizational Communication." Paper prepared for a course in Speech Communication, SUNY at Buffalo, October 1973. 16 pp. (ED 117 758).

Describes the use of an open systems approach in the investigation of information diffusion within an organization. Maintains that the use of this approach yields a better understanding of the communicative processes controlling an organization's activities.

Toomb, K., and others. "A Systems Model for Assessment and Diffusion." Paper presented at the Annual Meeting of the International Communication Association, Chicago, Ill., April 1975. 58 pp. (ED 120 885).

Examines the use of the Florida Assessment and Diffusion System (FADS) as a tool for effecting organizational change. Discusses five major FADS components: initiation, verification, problem solving, diffusion, evaluation, and documentation.

Walker, P. D. "Developing a Healthy Climate for Educational Change and administrative approach." *Community College Review*, Spring 1981, *8* (4), 22-27.

Finds three areas of faculty/administrator interaction to have the greatest impact on organizational climate: goal setting and internal governance, application of resources, and organizational and personal development. Suggests strategies under each area for promoting a positive climate.